First published 1975
Published by
William Collins Sons and Company Limited,
Glasgow and London
© 1975 The Scottish Milk Marketing Board
Printed in Great Britain
ISBN 0 00 435186 X

Make More of Milk

Edited by
Elizabeth MacIntosh

Published by William Collins Sons and Company Limited
on behalf of the Scottish Milk Marketing Board

Contents

Introduction

Milk is such good value, both in terms of cost and with regard to its nutritional value, that it is a pity not to make the most of it. Housewives have an eye for a bargain, and their consumption of milk in recent years has increased dramatically.

The Scottish Milk Marketing Board has, therefore, been encouraged to produce a new recipe book which will help housewives to make the most of milk and dairy products.

Although housewives appreciate the value of milk, it is clear from questions they ask that there are a number of aspects of milk and dairy products where they feel they would like to know a bit more, and the opportunity has been taken to present this in a simple but, hopefully, useful form.

The Scottish Milk Marketing Board acknowledges the assistance given by the staff and students of the Home and Food Studies Department of the Queen's College, Glasgow, who co-operated with the Board's own Home Economics Department in the preparation of this book.

Metric measures and oven temperatures have been used throughout the book, and *approximate* imperial equivalents are given. Conversions are based on 25g = 1 oz, 500 ml = 1 pint, 2·5 cm = 1 inch, in accordance with Standard British Practice. With larger amounts, quantities have been rounded up or down, and have been appropriately balanced.

Note to Parents
On pages 82–93, there is a section devoted to recipes for children to make themselves. Some safety hints are offered for children on page 82, but it should be stressed here too that children working in the kitchen should *always* be supervised. They should be taught how to cope with hot food and equipment in the safest possible way. And they should be trained to take the greatest care with boiling water and, even more so, with hot fat.

1. Your Pinta and its Relatives

With the advancement of science, a lot of the food we eat nowadays is processed and fortified, dehydrated then reconstituted, frozen then thawed, and many foods contain artificial preservatives, flavourings and colourings. However when you buy a pint of milk you can drink it to the last drop and absorb its natural goodness.

Milk is an important part of our diet from birth to retirement, and it is very important that at every stage in life we get a good supply of it.

When we are young it helps us to develop a healthy body and to build strong bones, teeth and nails. In our teens and twenties it will repair damaged tissues and help to give us plenty of energy. Through middle age it will soothe upset tummies, give us a quick pep up and fill the energy gap. As we get older, it will help to keep our bones strong. It is easily digestible and is excellent value for money as we can use every drop in the bottle.

It is the only food which contains all the nutrients which are necessary to maintain life and promote body growth. Proteins, fat, carbohydrates, mineral elements and vitamins are present in milk in well balanced proportions. They are in a form for immediate use by the body and there is no waste.

Milk

Although most milk retailers supply only one type of milk, most housewives are aware that there are a number of different types on the market. All milk sold has to conform to certain requirements and will come under one of the legal designations. It may be helpful to know what the different types are.

Pasteurised Milk
Milk which has been heated to not less than 63°C (145°F) for at least 30 minutes or, more usually, 72°C (161°F) for 15 seconds, and then cooled to a temperature of not more than 7·2°C (45°F). This is the milk most widely retailed throughout Scotland and accounts for 86% of all milk sold.

Premium Milk
Untreated milk which immediately after production has been cooled to 7·2°C (45°F) and put into retail containers. The temperature is not allowed to exceed 10°C (50°F). This type of milk accounts for only 5% of all liquid milk produced in Scotland.

Homogenized Milk
This is pasteurised milk which by mechanical means has had the butterfat globules dispersed throughout the milk. There is no cream line with homogenized milk, since the butterfat cannot rise to the surface. This type of milk is mostly supplied in bulk form as 13·6 or 22·7 litre (3 or 5 gallon) packs. It is placed in a refrigerated dispenser and is generally found in cafés, restaurants, hospitals, and canteens.

Sterilised Milk
This is homogenised milk which has been filled into bottles which are capped and then heated to a temperature of not less than 100°C (212°F) and held at this temperature for a sufficient period of time. It is very rare in Scotland.

U.H.T. Milk
The ultra heat treatment of milk is similar to pasteurisation but the milk is heated to not less than 132°C (270°F) for at least one second. The milk is packed in cartons in sterile conditions and will keep for up to 3 months without refrigeration.

Channel Islands Milk
This is the milk from a cow of the Jersey, Guernsey, or South Devon breeds, which must not contain less than 4% butterfat. It is a very creamy milk, but not retailed widely in Scotland.

Undesignated Milk
This milk is only sold in some sparsely populated rural areas. There is no standard laid down for such milk, but the quantity involved is very small.

Identifying Milk
It will be compulsory by 1976 to use caps of different colours for different types of milk.

Pasteurised	– Silver
Premium	– Green with a gold lattice
Standard	– Plain green
Homogenized	– Red
Channel Islands, Pasteurised	– Gold
Channel Islands, Unpasteurised	– Green with gold stripe
Undesignated	– Cerise
Kosher	– Blue with silver stripe

Nutrients in Milk

568 ml (1 pint) of milk will supply nearly one quarter of the protein and nearly nine tenths of the calcium required daily for a moderately active man.

Approximate composition of 568 ml (1 pint) of milk:

Protein	19 grams
Fat	22 grams
Carbohydrate	26 grams
Calcium	702 milligrams
Iron	150 milligrams
Vitamin A	826 International Units (summer value)
	619 International Units (winter value)
Thiamiene (vitamin B.1)	0·2 milligrams
Riboflavine (vitamin B.2)	0·8 milligrams
Niacin (vitamin B Group)	0·3 milligrams
Vitamin C	12 milligrams
Vitamin B	8 International Units (summer value)
	2 International Units (winter value)

Packaging of Milk

Most milk still comes in the familiar and popular glass bottle, but in some situations a returnable container is not very suitable, so the dairy industry has developed different types of non-returnable packaging. The most widely used is the carton, which comes in many shapes and sizes, ranging from the single-portion jigger pack you sometimes see in restaurants to the 1·14 litre (2 pint) carton familiar in shops and supermarkets. Most cartons are made of cardboard with a poly-thene lining, but some are made completely of plastic. There is also a considerable quantity of milk packed in plastic sachets.

For use in catering establishments, milk is packed in 13·6 and 22·7 litre (3 and 5 gallon) cartons which fit neatly into refrigerated milk dispensers, so that you always get your milk cool and fresh.

Children and Milk

There are some children who don't like milk straight from the bottle, but as milk is such a valuable food it is very important that all children have milk in some form or another. There are many ways of encouraging children to drink milk. Commercial flavourings and powders can be added to milk which change the flavour and the colour, but not the nutritional value. The syrups and powders come in many different flavours and can be used at the desired strength. Hot milk drinks are also a good way of getting children to take milk and if a child is ill this is an excellent way to build up his strength again. As milk contains so many nutrients especially impor-tant to a growing child it is worthwhile considering the many different ways in which this can be included in the diet. Cereals and porridge, hot drinks, coffee, soup, rice and other milk puddings, flans, milk jelly and custard are some ways in which milk can be included in the diet. Recipes for milk drinks are on page 81.

Milk for the Invalid and the Convalescent

Milk is of great value in the diet of invalids and convalescents because of its high food value. A good way to aid recovery is to give the most nutritious and most easily digestible food so that the body can benefit with the least effort, and milk is a good source of vitamins and calcium. Food should be very carefully cooked, portions should be small and the tray for the individual should be fresh and neatly set. Dishes such as junket, milky soups and even small sponge cakes with a little cream will be both nourishing and tempting.

Fresh Dairy Cream

Cream is produced from the part of the cow's milk which is rich in fat. This has been separated from the milk by skimming or other means. In modern manufacture the cream is separated by centrifugal force in a mechanical separator rather like a spin-dryer. The cream, which is lighter, flows towards the centre while the heavier skimmed milk is thrown towards the outside edge of the plate. The cream and skimmed milk are collected from two different outlet pipes. There are strict legal standards which must be maintained by producers handling cream. Types of cream are defined principally by the percentage of fat which they contain. The legal minimum for each category is:

Half cream	12%
Single cream	18%
Sterilised cream	23%
Whipping cream	35%
Double cream	48%
Clotted cream	55%

Single Cream
This is a pouring cream and is ideal for coffee, porridge, cereals or fruit. Pour a little into soup after serving to give extra creaminess. Pour cream over either hot or cold sweets for added richness. Mouth-watering salad dressing can be made with single cream (see page 33). It can be added to sauces and stews to make them absolutely delicious. It will not whip.

Half Cream
A thin cream to serve with coffee.

Whipping Cream
As the name suggests, this is ideal for whipping and can be used in many ways for filling pastries and decorating cakes and desserts.

Double Cream
This is a rich cream which will float on the top of coffee or soup. This cream will whip but before whipping a little milk can be added to make it go further.

Ultra Heat Treated Cream
Ultra Heat Treated cream (or U.H.T. cream as it is known) comes in two types, single cream and whipping cream. This cream can be bought in 170 ml ($\frac{1}{3}$ pint) packs and can be kept without refrigeration for up to 12 weeks. As it's so easy to store it is very handy to keep some in the house for unexpected occasions.

Soured Cream

This is made from a single cream which has a culture added to it. It has a sharp refreshing taste and gives a special flavour to your cooking. It makes a super dressing for a salad and gives an excellent flavour to sauces or stews, but in some parts of Scotland it is not always easy to obtain. Fresh cream can be soured by adding one teaspoonful of lemon juice to a 140 g (5 oz) carton of cream.

Clotted Cream

Clotted cream is a cream rich in fat, about 48%–55% which after processing has a crumbly texture. This cream is a speciality in Cornwall and Devon where clotted cream teas are served. These consist of scones with strawberry jam topped with clotted cream. They make an excellent afternoon tea.

Sterilised Cream

This cream is heated to a very high temperature 104–110°C (219–230°F) for 20 minutes and cooled slowly. As a result of this process, the cream may have a slightly caramelised flavour. It is packed in tins or bottles and will keep indefinitely.

Storage of Cream

Keep cream in its original container as this has been sterilised. Keep it cool and covered, preferably in a refrigerator stored away from food which may taint it, like fish or onions.

Whipping and Piping Cream

The cream used should be whipping or double cream.

The cream and all the utensils to be used should be cold.

Whisk the cream in a bowl, using a rotary whisk until it begins to thicken in the centre, then stir with the whisk until all the cream is firm, but not stiff. Place the cream in a piping bag and decorate as required.

Butter

It takes about 8½ litres (18 pints) of milk to make 400 g (1 lb) of butter! Butter usually consists of about 81% butterfat and so has a relatively high calorie content, approximately 226 calories per ounce. It contains vitamins A and D and a small amount of protein, sugar (lactose) and minerals. Butter should be kept cool and away from any food with strong flavours and smells. Like milk it is affected by light and should be stored in a dark place. Butter comes in two main types, salt and unsalted. Salt butter will last longer than fresh, but it is largely a matter of preference as to which one you use. Butter is still a lot cheaper to buy in Britain than on the Continent and for cooking certain dishes butter is a must. A knob of butter placed on top of a steak before grilling makes it much tastier. The flavour of shortbread is definitely enhanced by using butter. Rich fruit cakes taste better and will keep longer if butter is used in baking them.

Scottish Cheeses

Cheese has been made in Scotland for centuries. Each farm had its own recipe for cheese, and some of these recipes have been handed down from generation to generation. The recipes are still followed today and although the cheese is produced by modern methods, they still retain the original flavour. The Scottish rainfall may not be very popular, but it produces lush pastures with first class grazing for cattle. The combination of fine cattle and good pasture results in quality milk particularly suited for making cheese.

The most popular cheese in Scotland is Scottish cheddar which is used in cooking, in salads, in sandwiches and with biscuits. It is a hard cheese matured for between 4 and 9 months and can be bought pre-packed or in a piece. It is manufactured as red or white cheddar, the difference being that to the red a harmless vegetable dye has been added. This gives the cheese a better colour for cooking. Some people seem to think that white cheese is stronger than red, or vice versa, but the strength of the cheese depends on the length of time it has been matured, and not on the colour.

Some of the islands still make their own cheeses. The islands of Arran, Islay and Orkney make individual Dunlop cheeses either white or coloured and one of the Orkney cheeses is smoked. Dunlop cheese is similar to cheddar, but is hand pressed and is a little softer and mellower.

Crowdie is a soft cheese which is still a favourite cheese in Scotland. It is excellent with bannocks and oatcakes and is available with cream added to it or wild garlic and herbs.

Cottage cheese is a very popular cheese especially with people on slimming diets. On its own or mixed with pineapple or tuna fish it makes a most tempting salad.

There are over thirty cheeses made in Scotland. Most of the recipes have been handed down from generation to generation and provide tremendous variety. Apart from the hard cheddar types of cheese, which themselves vary a great deal in flavour and texture, there is a large number of soft, special cheeses. Some are based originally on French types such as Brie and Camembert, and others are purely Scottish, like the soft cream cheese sold rolled in oatmeal.

Yogurt

Yogurt has long been a traditional food of the peoples of the Balkans and Middle East. It has been used for centuries for its therapeutic qualities, the medical profession recognising its use in cases of minor intestinal ailments.

Interest in yogurt spread to Italy, France, the Netherlands and many other European countries, and in the last 15 years has become popular in Britain largely because of the increasing interest in health foods and as a result of Continental travel. Scotland consumes around 40 million cartons of yogurt a year now.

There are two types of yogurt. Set yogurt has a firm surface, and stirred yogurt has a softer consistency. Yogurt can be made from whole or skimmed milk.

Apart from a little natural yogurt, practically all the yogurt sold commercially has fruit added to it. These yogurts are generally eaten just as they are, as a snack or as a dessert.

Natural yogurt can be eaten as it comes or used to enhance other foods. It can be used in sauces for fish or poultry and as a substitute for cream in baking and cold sweets.

Yogurt made from skimmed milk is also useful in cooking for people on low fat diets as it is nutritious as well as low in fat.

You can easily make yogurt at home. It may be difficult to obtain a 'starter' but it is simple to use a carton of bought yogurt for this purpose.

Flavouring	Amount used for (1 litre or 2 pints) of yogurt	Amount used for (125 ml or $\frac{1}{4}$ pint) of yogurt
Fruit – canned	1 small can	1 tablespoon
Fruit – fresh e.g. strawberries	200 g (8 oz)	$\frac{1}{2}$ pear or $\frac{1}{2}$ apple
Fruit – frozen (thawed)	159 g (6 oz)	1 tablespoon
Fruit juices from canned fruit if liked, or blackcurrant or orange juice	3–4 tablespoons	1 dessertspoon
Milk shake flavourings, coffee or cocoa powder	2–3 tablespoons (blended)	2–3 tablespoons (blended)
Essences	1–2 teaspoons	a few drops
Nuts	to taste	to taste
Sweetener (if wanted)		
Sugar	2 tablespoons	1 teaspoon
Saccharin	8 tablets	1 tablet
Honey	as sugar (use only after yogurt is made)	
Syrup	as sugar (use only after yogurt is made)	

Home Made Soft Yogurt

500 ml (1 pint) pasteurised milk
1 teaspoon sugar (if further
    sweetening e.g. jam or honey
    is not used)
1 carton (125 g or 5 oz) natural
    yogurt

1. Warm the milk to blood heat (36°C, 98°F).
2. Remove from heat and stir in sugar.
3. Gently whisk in yogurt with a wire whisk or a fork.
4. Transfer to a bowl and cover.
5. Leave in a warm place for 8–12 hours, or until set.
6. If cold yogurt is preferred refrigerate after setting.

Yield Approximately $\frac{3}{4}$ litre ($1\frac{1}{4}$ pints).

Once the yogurt has set, it is ready for use, either as it is, or with the addition of fruit or flavouring.

For firmer yogurt use UHT milk.

For low fat yogurt use skimmed milk with 1 dessertspoon instant milk powder added when warm.

For flavoured yogurt, add either a fruit flavour or jam. The use of jam adds a touch of colour to the yogurt. The addition of 1 dessertspoon honey makes a delicious yogurt.

For fruit yogurt, add small pieces of fresh, canned or thawed frozen fruit.

Interesting combinations can be made – chocolate and mint or coffee and walnut. You can add the flavouring before or after the yogurt is made. If you add the flavouring *after* the yogurt is made every member of the family can have his or her favourite flavour.

Some suggestions and quantities are given opposite.

Storage of Dairy Products without a Refrigerator

Milk, Cream and Yogurt

Stand in bowl of cold water in cool place. Cover with wet muslin, allowing each end to dip into water.

If opened, pour into shallow dish, rather than jug, cover with wet muslin.

Stand in earthenware or stone jar of water. Leave in cool place, on slate or marble if possible.

Butter

Place in bowl which is inside a second bowl full of cold water. Place inverted pottery flower pot over the top. Best if kept in current of air.

Cheese

Wrap in foil or perforated polythene and place in ventilated container away from milk and butter.

There is a special cheese box available which stops cheese sweating.

Keep some grated cheese in a jar in the store cupboard or in your freezer. It is then convenient for adding to sauces, soups and salads.

Removal of milk and milk produce stains

Milk and its products produce protein and greasy stains which, with proper treatment, can be easily removed.

The washing products containing enzymes remove most milky stains when the article is given a long soak in hand hot water followed by the appropriate wash. However, some milk stains require different treatment, especially in the case of a dry-clean garment.

Stains	Washable	Dry-clean
Milk	Soak article in cold water. Wash in normal way. Use a washing product containing enzymes	Use a grease solvent e.g. carbon tetrochloride
Chocolate or Cocoa	Scrape off excess. Wash in warm water and borax, then wash in usual way. Alternatively enzyme soak may be sufficient	Scrape off excess, treat with solvent and sponge with clean water
Milky Coffee	Treat with grease solvent before soaking and washing	As Chocolate
Ice Cream	Remove built up parts and soak in a suitable warm wash solution. If a greasy stain remains after fabric is dry, test with a solvent	As Chocolate
Tea with Milk	Soak in a suitable washing solution followed by rinsing. If stain is set and fabric is suitable use a high temperature washing method	As Chocolate
Cream	Fresh cream comes off with luke warm water. Dried cream may be removed by soaking in an enzyme product	As Chocolate

2. Home Freezing

Freezing is one of the newest ways of preserving food in the home.

The first necessity, of course, is the freezer. There are two types, the chest or top opening, and the upright or front opening type. The choice is yours, but bear in mind the space you have available. Obviously the upright freezer will occupy less space but its size is limited to the height which you can reach. The upright is also available as part of a refrigerator which is ideal for a smallish family with little space.

The chest type is more economical to run as the cold air does not escape when the freezer is opened but it can be more difficult to keep tidy and the baskets are heavy to lift when filled.

The size you will require depends on the number in the family and the amount of use you are going to have for the freezer. 28 cubic cm (1 cubic ft) holds 12 kg (25 lb) of food (in neat packages). This amount may seem a great deal but when you start buying in bulk or freezing garden produce you will find that you will need at least 56 cubic cm (2 cubic ft) for each member of the family.

How does a freezer preserve food?

If you look at the thermometer below you can compare the temperature in the freezer with the temperature in the refrigerator. You can see how much colder the freezer is. The lower the temperature the faster the food will freeze and the better the food will keep. Quick freezing produces foods which when thawed have little drip and are therefore better in flavour and texture. To achieve good results only freeze one tenth of the total capacity of the freezer at one time i.e. a 282 cubic cm (10 cubic ft) freezer could hold 125 kg (250 lb) frozen food but only 12 kg (25 lb) fresh food should be frozen at once.

It is important when freezing food to freeze only top quality fresh foods. These should be prepared as quickly and as hygienically as possible.

The bacteria which cause the food to spoil are not killed at low temperatures, they only stop growing. However, when the food is thawing the bacteria will begin to multiply just as they do on fresh foods. This is why it is important that there is as little bacteria as possible on the food before it is frozen and also why frozen foods, once thawed, should not be refrozen.

How long will food keep in the freezer?

This depends on a number of factors firstly the quality of the food frozen, how well it has been packed, i.e. the covering and the way air has been excluded. The more air and fat in the food the less time the food will keep. For instance, pork will keep for a shorter time than beef because of the fat in it. You should try to use food up so that it is not left too long in the freezer.

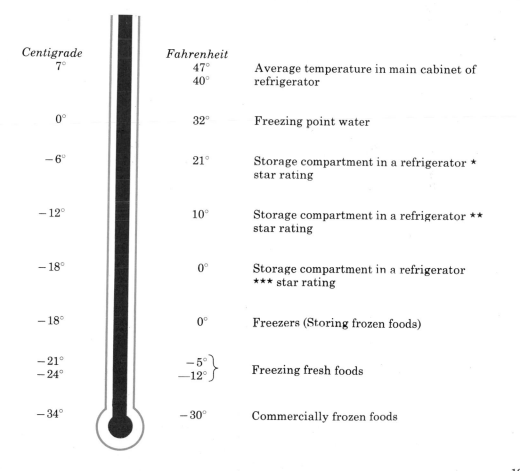

Centigrade	Fahrenheit	
7°	47°	Average temperature in main cabinet of
	40°	refrigerator
0°	32°	Freezing point water
−6°	21°	Storage compartment in a refrigerator ★ star rating
−12°	10°	Storage compartment in a refrigerator ★★ star rating
−18°	0°	Storage compartment in a refrigerator ★★★ star rating
−18°	0°	Freezers (Storing frozen foods)
−21° −24°	−5° −12°	Freezing fresh foods
−34°	−30°	Commercially frozen foods

Vegetables and fruit – can keep up to a year
Beef   – 6–9 months
Mutton   – 6 months
Pork   – 3–4 months
Made-up dishes – 2–3 months
Baking   – 1 year

The above is merely a rough guide as you will be given a more comprehensive list with your new freezer.

If your idea in buying a freezer is to economise there is no point in buying many expensive containers at one time. These are best collected gradually as you find out what your needs are.

Buy good quality containers as some of the cheaper ones tend to crack at low temperatures in the freezer. Keep any containers – even tiny ones for jam or butter obtained in restaurants are ideal for chopped parsley or a single egg white.

All the foil dishes from 'carry-out' shops are ideal for storing stews, etc. The plastic boxes used to package produce such as mushrooms make good rigid containers for soft fruits. Even the plastic containers for soft drinks are good for cream and small amounts of liquids.

After washing, milk cartons can be used as 'formers' by slipping a polythene bag inside the carton and filling it with liquid such as soup. Put the carton in the freezer and when the food is frozen remove the polythene bag to give a neat package which is easy to store and takes up less space. The carton can be used again.

Polythene bags should be of a thick quality as smells can carry from one food to another if they are too thin. However, instead of trying to wash and dry good polythene a thin one can be slipped into the thicker one and the thin one discarded after use, the better quality bag being kept for re-use.

As with polythene bags, aluminium foil should be of a good thick quality; it is ideal for wrapping oddly shaped foods. These packages are better slipped into a polythene bag after wrapping as sometimes bones, etc., can puncture the foil and allow air into the package.

After wrapping, the foods have to be labelled. This is necessary as even if you think you will remember which is stewed meat and which is stewed rhubarb it can often be quite difficult to distinguish the different foods when they are frozen. Use labels which are moisture proof. Ordinary ones cannot be stuck on with Sellotape as this is not moisture proof – you can buy special tape for freezers. Write on the labels with a moisture proof pen and detail the type of food, date, quantity and any instructions, e.g. 'Stewed Apples, October 1975, 400 g (1 lb) no sugar added'. Fasten polythene bags either with tape or 'tie-tags' either of paper or plastic with wire inside, obviously the plastic ones last longer.

The picture shows how the top is twisted after removing as much air as possible, then turned over and the 'tie-tag' put on. This prevents air from getting into the bag. Never tie a knot in a bag unless you are going to throw the bag away after use.

Many people are afraid to freeze dairy produce. However experiments into the freezing of cream, cheese and butter, gave the following results:

Double Cream
The cream was prepared in the following way for the freezer and packed in polythene cartons. It was frozen for 3 months and then tested for consistency and flavour.

Sugar added to cream and cream whipped	Very successful
No sugar added to whipped cream	Not very successful
Unwhipped cream with and without sugar	Neither very successful even when beaten after freezing
Cream beaten and piped into stars frozen, with and without sugar	Both very successful

As you can see from the results it is advisable to whip the cream lightly with a little sugar (2 teaspoonfuls to 125 ml or $\frac{1}{4}$ pint) before freezing.

Scottish Cheese

A number of cheeses were tasted before freezing and then put in polythene bags and frozen for 3 months.
Cheddar cheese retained good flavour although it tended to be crumbly after thawing. Cheddar cheese grated before freezing was very successful.
Softer cheeses tended to develop a stronger flavour.

Scottish Butter

Butter freezes very well, especially butter which is double-wrapped with a greaseproof lining under the foil wrapper. Other butters would need to be over-wrapped before being frozen.

Some Hints for the Freezer

Put chopped mint or parsley in ice cube trays with a little water and freeze. Put in a bag when frozen and drop straight into soups or sauces when needed.

Egg whites can also be frozen in ice cube trays.

Cut green or red peppers into quarters, blanch, wrap individually in foil and freeze. Use in stews, goulash etc.

Freeze raspberries or other soft fruits separately in a little sugar and use to decorate soufflés or gâteaux.

Freezer Raspberry Jam

500 g (1¼ lb) raspberries
800 g (2 lb) castor sugar
½ bottle Certo
2 tablespoons lemon juice

1. Put raspberries and sugar in a bowl and leave for 1 hour, stirring occasionally until the sugar has dissolved.
2. Add ½ bottle Certo and the lemon juice.
3. Stir for 2 minutes.
4. Pour into small dry jars and leave 1 cm (½ inch) head space.
5. Cover well and leave in a warm place for 48 hours.
6. Freeze.
N.B. Keeps well for 6 months.

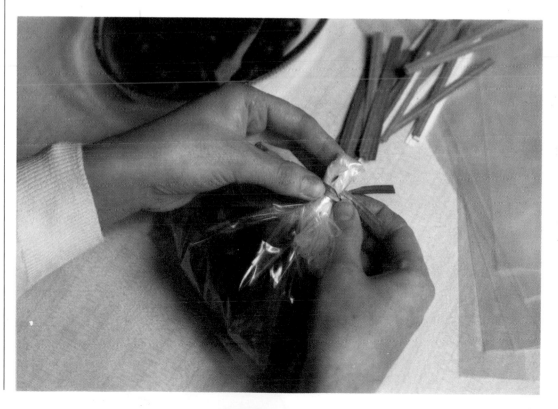

Some foods do not freeze well and these should be avoided especially in made-up dishes. The following are some examples:

Food	Results
Bacon	Salty, fishy flavour. Tends to toughen in casseroles.
Garlic and Peppers	Both develop very strong flavours and are better added after freezing.
Vanilla Essence	This can develop unpleasant flavours but if a vanilla pod is used it is much better.
Mayonnaise	Separates
Sauces and soups thickened with flour	These separate. Corn-flour is better than flour though it still separates.
Hardboiled egg	Spongy result.
Yolks of egg	These toughen on freezing though they can be mixed with a pinch of sugar or salt and this helps a little. However whites freeze very satisfactorily.
Tomatoes	These go soft and soggy and are not suitable for garnishes or salads but are good for soups and sauces.

3. Entertaining at Home

Having a party can be great fun if you follow a few simple rules and plan ahead. With good organisation you will have plenty of energy left to enjoy the party yourself!

First of all write down a list of the different dishes which you are going to make. From this list make out a shopping list and order any items which might take the shop a day or two to supply. Work out the preparation of each dish and do as much as possible the day before or even earlier.

Think of how you are going to decorate the house and do this as far in advance as you can.

Find all the serving dishes you require and if necessary wash or polish them.

As you complete items which have to be done tick them off on the list. This gives you an idea how much you still have to do and at what pace you have to work.

It is advisable not to try out a new dish for a party. If you want to do a dish that you haven't made before try it out at least once so that you know how to make it and how long it will take to prepare.

Don't undertake too many dishes which take ages to prepare. In fact, if you can avoid it, don't make any that involve a lot of preparation.

Cheese and Wine Party

This is an easy way of feeding a large number of people. It is also a good way of mixing people who don't know each other very well. There are a number of different types of food which you can supply at a cheese and wine party, such as creamy dips and savoury biscuits spread with butter and garnished with various cheeses and pickles. Cheese and fruit or cheese and pickles are popular spiked onto cocktail sticks: allow 45–55 g (1½–2 oz) cheese per person. Cheese straws are always very acceptable and you can make savoury pastry dishes in the form of flans. You can augment your food with crisps and nuts and some of the many packets of savouries which are available from the shops.

One of the problems with the food for a cheese and wine party is that some of the food has to be prepared just before your guests arrive. Savoury flans, dips and pastry dishes can be made ahead, but garnished savoury biscuits will tend to go soft after an hour or so. Dips can be made and kept in the refrigerator for up to 24 hours beforehand and cheese straws can be stored in an airtight tin.

Make an attractive centrepiece with a cheese board containing a wide range of Scottish cheeses. Apples, grapes and oranges add a splash of colour to your cheese display.

The wine for a cheese and wine party depends very much on your palate and in all probability your bank balance! There are many good inexpensive wines which can be bought. Your local wine merchant will be able to advise you on the best wines to serve.

Photograph shows Savoury Flan (page 28), Savoury Cheese Slice (page 28), Mushroom and Ham Dip (page 25), Cheddar Cheese Boats (page 29), Cheese and fruit on Cocktail Sticks, Savoury Cheese Tartlets (page 27), Curried Dip (page 26), Cheese and Pineapple Dip (page 26), Cheese Fondue (page 29).

Cottage Cheese and Bacon Dip

100 g (4 oz) bacon
200 g (8 oz) cottage cheese
1–2 level teaspoons finely grated
  onion
parsley

1. Grill bacon and chop into small pieces; leave to cool.
2. Mix cottage cheese, onion and bacon thoroughly.
3. Place in serving dish and garnish with parsley.

Mushroom and Ham Dip

50 g (2 oz) lean ham
125 ml (¼ pint) fresh double cream
1 (125 g or 5 oz) carton natural
  yogurt
1 medium (298 g or 10½ oz) can
  condensed mushroom soup
cayenne pepper to garnish

1. Grill ham and chop up.
2. Lightly whip cream.
3. Stir in yogurt and soup, then ham.
4. Place in serving dish and garnish with cayenne pepper.

Curried Dip

200 g (8 oz) cream cheese
4 tablespoons mayonnaise
1 (125 g or 5 oz) carton natural
   yogurt
3–4 level teaspoons curry powder
salt to taste
3–4 tablespoons sultanas

1. Beat cheese until smooth together with mayonnaise and natural yogurt.
2. Stir in curry powder and season to taste.
3. Add 3 tablespoons sultanas and mix through.
4. Place in serving bowl and garnish with remaining sultanas.

Cheese and Pineapple Dip

200 g (8 oz) cottage cheese
4 tablespoons fresh single cream
4 tablespoons finely chopped
   canned pineapple
salt and cayenne pepper
chopped walnuts to garnish

1. Sieve cottage cheese, then beat till smooth.
2. Mix cottage cheese with cream and pineapple.
3. Season to taste with salt and a little cayenne pepper.
4. Transfer to a serving bowl and garnish with walnuts.

Party Cheese Dip

2 (75 g or 3 oz) packets cottage
   cheese
pinch of salt and pepper
3 tablespoons milk

Alternative Flavourings:
   small can shrimps, drained
   or chopped onion
   or chopped pineapple
   or chopped ham

1. Cream cheese and add seasoning slowly, blending with milk till smooth.
2. Add chopped shrimps, onion, pineapple or ham.
3. Serve with potato crisps, twiglets or crisp cheese biscuits.

Cheese Straws

100 g (4 oz) plain flour
$\frac{1}{4}$ level teaspoon dried mustard
$\frac{1}{4}$ level teaspoon salt
a little cayenne pepper
62 g (2$\frac{1}{4}$ oz) Scottish butter
75 g (3 oz) Scottish cheddar
   cheese, finely grated
1 egg yolk
2–3 teaspoons water

Oven temperature   180°C 350°F Mark 4
Position in oven   Centre
Time in oven   10–15 minutes

1. Sieve flour, mustard, salt and cayenne pepper together.
2. Rub in butter until the mixture is like fine breadcrumbs.
3. Stir in cheese with a fork.
4. Mix to a stiff dough with egg yolk and water.
5. Roll out pastry to 1 cm ($\frac{1}{2}$ inch) thick and cut into straw sizes. Make some rings of pastry also.
6. Bake in a hot oven until pale golden brown.
7. Cool on tray then arrange bundles of the cheese straws through a ring of pastry.

Savoury Balls

3 eggs
6 leaves of fresh chives, chopped
125 g (5 oz) cooked chicken
125 ml (¼ pint) mayonnaise
25 g (1 oz) breadcrumbs
125 g (5 oz) Scottish red cheddar
  cheese
1 small lettuce heart
2 tomatoes

Number of servings   12 balls

1. Hardboil the eggs, then chop them, and mix with the chives.
2. Mince the chicken, mix with the eggs and chives and add enough mayonnaise to bind.
3. Divide the mixture into twelve balls and roll lightly in breadcrumbs.
4. Finely grate 25 g (1 oz) of the cheese and sprinkle a little on top of each ball.
5. Slightly brown under the grill.
6. Make a bed of lettuce on a plate and place balls attractively on top.
7. Cut remaining cheese and the tomatoes into cubes and put onto cocktail sticks.
8. Arrange between the balls and scatter the remaining cubes in between balls.

Crunchy Cheese Bobs

37 g (1½ oz) Scottish butter
75 g (3 oz) Scottish cheddar
  cheese, grated
salt, pepper and dry mustard
1 packet potato crisps (crushed)
25 g (1 oz) breadcrumbs

1. Soften butter and beat in cheese, breadcrumbs and seasonings.
2. Form mixture into small balls and roll in crushed crisps.
3. Chill and serve on cocktail sticks.

Savoury Cheese Tartlets

Short crust pastry:
100 g (4 oz) plain flour
pinch of salt
25 g (1 oz) lard
25 g (1 oz) Scottish butter
1 tablespoon cold water to mix
Filling:
2 tomatoes
50 g (2 oz) bacon
1 egg, separated
12 g (½ oz) Scottish butter
1 level teaspoon cornflour
4 tablespoons milk
50 g (2 oz) Scottish cheddar
  cheese, grated
salt and pepper

Oven temperature   200°C 400°F Mark 6
Position in oven   Second shelf
Time in oven   20 minutes
Number of tartlets   12

1. Sieve flour and salt. Add fat and rub into flour until mixture resembles fine breadcrumbs. Add sufficient water to form a stiff dough. Knead lightly until smooth.
2. Roll out pastry and line 12 small patty tins. Bake 'blind' until half cooked.
3. Chop tomatoes and bacon, and fry bacon gently. Place on bottom of patty tins.
4. Beat egg yolk. Heat butter in pan, add cornflour and remove from heat. Blend in milk and egg yolk.
5. Stir in cheese and seasoning.
6. Whisk egg white until stiff and fold into cheese mixture. Spoon into patty cases, filling to three quarters full. Bake for 20 minutes and serve piping hot.

Savoury Flans

Cheese pastry:
100 g (4 oz) plain flour
salt, pepper and mustard
25 g (1 oz) lard
25 g (1 oz) Scottish butter
37 g (1½ oz) Scottish cheddar
    cheese, finely grated
1 tablespoon cold water (approx.)

Filling 1:
25 g (1 oz) bacon, chopped and
    cooked
50 g (2 oz) mushrooms, sliced and
    cooked
2 eggs
125 ml (¼ pint) milk
salt and pepper

Filling 2:
1 (80 g or 3¼ oz) can shrimps
50 g (2 oz) Scottish cheddar
    cheese, grated
1 tomato, sliced
2 eggs
125 ml (¼ pint) milk
salt and pepper

Oven temperature   190°C 375°F Mark 5
Position in oven   Top half
Time in oven   Total 45–50 minutes
Number of servings   6–8

1. Make up pastry by sieving flour and
seasonings together then rub in fats. Mix in
cheese then bind together with as little water
as possible.
2. Roll out pastry and line an 18 cm (7 inch)
flan ring. Bake 'blind' in a fairly hot oven for
15–20 minutes. (see above).
3. Place bacon and mushrooms (or shrimps,
cheese and tomato) in flan and cover with
eggs beaten up in milk. Season.
4. Bake in a warm oven (170°C 325°F Mark 3)
for about 30 minutes until egg is set.
    Serve either hot or cold.

Savoury Cheese Slice

75 g (3 oz) Scottish butter
200 g (8 oz) self raising flour, sieved
125 g (5 oz) Scottish cheddar
    cheese
1 egg
1 small onion, thinly sliced
50 g (2 oz) mushrooms, peeled and
    chopped
100 g (4 oz) streaky bacon,
    chopped
pinch mixed herbs
salt and pepper
milk if necessary

Oven temperature   200°C 400°F Mark 6
Position in oven   ⅓ from top
Time in oven   20 minutes
Number of slices   18

1. Rub 50 g (2 oz) of the butter into the flour
until it resembles breadcrumbs.
2. Stir in 75 g (3 oz) of the cheese then mix
to a fairly soft dough with the egg and some
milk if necessary.
3. Fry the onion, mushrooms and bacon
gently for about 5 minutes in the remaining
25 g (1 oz) butter.
4. Divide dough into 2 pieces and roll out
each piece into a 20 cm (8 inch) square.
5. Place one on a greased baking sheet,
cover with onion, mushrooms and bacon,
then sprinkle with herbs and seasoning.
6. Damp edges and cover with second piece
of dough. Press to seal edges together.
7. Brush with milk and sprinkle with remaining cheese.
8. Bake towards the top of a fairly hot oven
for about 20 minutes until crisp and golden.
9. Serve cut into fingers or wedges. May be
eaten hot or cold.

Cheddar Cheese Boats

100 g (4 oz) short crust pastry
2–3 tablespoons apple purée
pinch of cinnamon
100 g (4 oz) Scottish cheddar
   cheese, grated
2–3 tablespoons fresh double
   cream
salt and pepper
dash of Worcestershire sauce
3 tomatoes

1. Line boat shaped patty tins with pastry and bake 'blind'. Leave to cool.
2. Flavour apple purée with cinnamon and put a little in the base of each boat.
3. Beat grated cheese, cream, seasoning and Worcestershire sauce together.
4. Fill boats with the cheese mixture.
5. Divide the tomatoes in 4 or 6 depending on the size and remove seeds. Make a sail for each boat by placing a cocktail stick through the tomatoes and into the boat.

Cheese Fondue

little butter
1 clove garlic
250 ml (½ pint) dry white wine
400 g (1 lb) Scottish cheddar
   cheese, grated
pinch of cayenne pepper
salt
1 level tablespoon cornflour

1. Butter the bottom and sides of a fireproof dish or double saucepan.
2. Rub round dish with cut clove of garlic.
3. Pour the wine into the dish, reserving a little for blending with the cornflour.
4. Toss in the grated cheese and stir over a gentle heat until the cheese has melted. Season.
5. Add the blended cornflour and stir well until it has thickened and simmered for 3 minutes.
6. Keep warm over gentle heat stirring occasionally
7. Serve with cubes of crusty French bread or toast, which are speared on a fork and dipped in the fondue.

Buffet Party

A buffet party is an easier way of entertaining a number of people than giving a dinner party. The buffet can be done quite simply or it can be very elaborate.

For a simple buffet party a selection of fruit juices or melon can be used as a starter, followed by various cold meats and salad. If you have a good butcher ask him to slice the exact number of slices of meat you require as this saves a lot of time and can be more economical. The sweet can be your own particular favourite cold sweet augmented with ice cream, fresh fruit salad and cream. You can round off your party with a selection of Scottish cheeses served with butter and biscuits, accompanied by coffee and cream.

For a more elaborate buffet party your starters could be pâté which can be bought in a shop or made at home, if you are more adventurous. There is also a recipe in this book for prawn cocktail which is always a favourite starter. These are more expensive dishes, but are very popular. If you wish to cook your own meat there is a vast selection of meats, poultry and game to choose from for your buffet table. There is also a wide range of sweets which are suitable for a buffet party. Sweets served in individual dishes look better than, perhaps, one large trifle or flan which will have lost its appearance by the time a few people have helped themselves and will avoid a situation where the last to appear are left with the scrapings.

Photograph shows Oriental Egg Salad (page 33), Buffet Salad (page 33), Summer Salad (page 31), Consommé Eggs (page 32), Tuna Fish and Cheese Salad (page 31), Ginger Creams (page 32), Fresh Fruit Salad, Party Mandarin Cheesecake (page 32), Bavarian Cream (page 33).

Summer Salad

Dressing:
125 ml (¼ pint) fresh double cream
little mayonnaise
salt and pepper

100 g (4 oz) Scottish red cheddar cheese
1 small (198 g or 7 oz) can luncheon meat
few black grapes
few green grapes
1 red apple
lettuce
tomato for garnish

Number of servings 4

Dressing:
1. Whisk cream lightly and add mayonnaise and seasoning.
2. Cut cheese and luncheon meat into cubes and add to dressing.
3. Wash grapes, then halve and remove stones.
4. Core apple and cut into cubes.
5. Add fruit and toss ingredients in dressing.
6. Serve on a bed of lettuce. Garnish with tomato and grapes.

Tuna Fish and Cheese Salad

1 small (100 g or 4 oz) carton cottage cheese
1 small (87 g or 3½ oz) can tuna fish
lettuce
1 small can pineapple slices
salt and pepper
cucumber slices

1. Mix cottage cheese and fish together, season.
2. Spoon onto drained pineapple slices.
3. Serve on bed of lettuce and garnish with cucumber.

Party Mandarin Cheesecake

3 eggs, separated
75 g (3 oz) castor sugar
1 small (150 g or 6 oz) can orange
  juice
1½ level tablespoons powdered
  gelatine
200 g (8 oz) Scottish cheddar
  cheese, finely grated
125 ml (¼ pint) milk
125 ml (¼ pint) fresh single cream
125 ml (¼ pint) fresh double cream
1 medium (312 g or 11 oz) can
  mandarin oranges, drained

Number of servings   6–8

1. Whisk egg yolks, sugar and half of the orange juice together in a basin over a pan of hot water till thickened.
2. Put gelatine and remaining orange juice into a small saucepan and stir over a low heat till gelatine has dissolved.
3. Mix together cheese and milk in a basin.
4. Whip single and double creams together till thickened but not stiff and add to the cheese.
5. Chop half of the mandarins, add to cheese mixture and stir into thickened egg yolk mixture. Gradually add gelatine stirring well.
6. Finally fold in stiffly beaten egg whites.
7. Pour into serving dish and leave to set.

Ginger Creams

250 ml (½ pint) fresh double cream
8 level tablespoons ginger
  marmalade
25 g (1 oz) castor sugar
a little advocaat – optional
4 egg whites
chopped nuts

Number of servings   10–12

1. Whip cream until stiff then fold in ginger marmalade, sugar and advocaat.
2. Beat egg whites until stiff and fold together with cream mixture.
3. Serve in individual sweet dishes and decorate with chopped nuts.

Consommé Eggs

1 medium (425 g or 15 oz) can
  concentrated consommé soup
9 eggs
250 ml (½ pint) fresh double cream
salt and pepper
sliced hardboiled egg and parsley
  to garnish

Number of servings   8–10

1. Place can of soup in refrigerator several hours before using.
2. Hardboil eggs, shell and chop them.
3. Whisk fresh cream until fairly stiff. Season with salt and pepper.
4. Add eggs to cream and mix well. Place mixture in a shallow dish and spread over base.
5. Pour consommé over egg mixture.
6. Garnish with sliced hardboiled egg and parsley.

Cream and Mayonnaise Dressing

125 ml (¼ pint) fresh double cream
2 tablespoons mayonnaise
salt and pepper

1. Beat cream lightly and add mayonnaise
and salt and pepper. Serve as an accompaniment to a salad.

Fresh Cream Dressing

3 syboes (spring onions)
125 ml (¼ pint) fresh double cream
salt and pepper
little lemon juice

1. Wash and finely slice syboes.
2. Whisk cream lightly and add salt and
pepper, lemon juice and syboes.
3. Serve as an accompaniment to a salad.

Oriental Egg Salad

50 g (2 oz) long grain rice
2 eggs, hardboiled
½ stick celery
125 ml (¼ pint) fresh double cream
salt and pepper
2 tablespoons syboes, chopped
50 g (2 oz) raisins
100 g (4 oz) Scottish cheddar
    cheese, grated

Number of servings   3–4

1. Cook rice in fast boiling, salted water
for 12 minutes, drain. Rinse with cold water.
Drain thoroughly.
2. Hardboil eggs and chop them up, keeping
½ egg for garnish.
3. Wash and chop up celery.
4. Beat cream lightly and add seasoning and
syboes.
5. Add rice, raisins, grated cheese, celery
and chopped hardboiled egg.
6. Serve in a bowl garnished with egg and
raisins.

Buffet Salad

125 ml (¼ pint) fresh double cream
2 red apples, chopped
100 g (4 oz) Scottish cheddar
    cheese, cubed
100 g (4 oz) ham, cubed
1 small can peaches, cubed
50 g (2 oz) salted peanuts
50 g (2 oz) sultanas
1 lettuce
cucumber and tomato to garnish

Number of servings   4

1. Lightly whip cream.
2. Mix in apples, cheese, ham, peaches, nuts
and sultanas.
3. Serve on bed of lettuce.
4. Garnish with tomato and cucumber.

Bavarian Cream

12 egg yolks
300 g (12 oz) sugar
750 ml (1½ pints) milk
1½ teaspoons vanilla essence
37 g (1½ oz) powdered gelatine
6 tablespoons cold water
375 ml (¾ pint) fresh double cream
150 g (6 oz) walnuts, chopped

Number of servings   12

1. Beat the egg yolks and sugar until smooth
in top of double boiler.
2. Heat milk and add to egg yolk mixture then
add vanilla and place over boiling water. Stir
until the mixture is smooth and thick, remove
from heat.
3. Sprinkle the gelatine in the cold water in
a cup. Place in a pan of warm water and heat
gently until gelatine dissolves.
4. Add the gelatine to egg mixture.
5. Allow the egg custard to cool.
6. Beat cream until stiff and add most of the
cream and nuts to the custard.
7. Pour into individual dishes and decorate
with remaining cream and walnuts.
N.B. Use up egg whites either by making
meringues, or with recipe like Ginger Creams
on page 32.

Children's Party

A birthday party is a must for most children and is the highlight of the birthday fun. To save washing-up and avoid breakages it is a good idea to use paper plates, sweet dishes and napkins. Mugs for drinks are safer and more stable than glass or plastic tumblers.

At the table have a set place for each child with his or her name at it, either written out in cream cheese on a sandwich or on a small cake written in butter icing – pink for the girls and blue for the boys. Sausages on sticks or cubes of cheese on sticks are popular and can be made into a hedgehog or monster. Children will want to try most things, so keep servings, cakes and biscuits small.

Flavoured milk drinks can be served and are cheaper and far more nutritious than lemonade and will not upset the child's digestion. Milk shake syrup or powder can be added to milk to give attractive pastel colours. Serve milk in glass jugs. When catering for younger children who haven't got too big an appetite, the birthday cake can be kept on the table as a centrepiece and cut and wrapped up to take home along with perhaps a balloon and a small bar of chocolate.

Ice cream may be served at a separate time from the meal with perhaps some mandarin oranges or pineapple pieces and cream.

Photograph shows Sandwich Gâteau (page 36), Party Cheese Scones (page 36), Peach Ships Ahoy! (page 37), Kitten Cake (page 38), Cheese Fingers (page 35), Individual Sponges (page 37).

Cheese Fingers

1 (187 g or 7½ oz) packet puff
   pastry
50 g (2 oz) Scottish cheddar
   cheese, grated
25 g (1 oz) Scottish butter, melted
1 egg
salt and pepper
a little milk

Oven temperature   220°C 425°F Mark 7
Position in oven   Centre
Time in oven   20–30 minutes
Number of servings   10–12

1. Roll out pastry and divide into two squares.
2. Lay one square on baking tin.
3. Mix cheese, butter, egg and seasoning for filling and spread on pastry.
4. Wet edges and lay on second square of pastry.
5. Brush with milk and bake in hot oven till golden brown. Serve cut into fingers.
6. Extras can be added to the basic filling, if desired. Add 2 hardboiled eggs, 50 g (2 oz) of either chopped, cooked meat or flaked white fish.

Sandwich Gâteau

1 small white loaf ⎱ same size
1 small brown loaf ⎰ approximately
butter for spreading

Filling 1:
2 eggs, hardboiled
knob of butter
mayonnaise
chopped chives
salt and pepper

Mash all the ingredients together, season well.

Filling 2:
2 tomatoes
100 g (4 oz) corned beef
2–3 teaspoons H.P. sauce
salt and pepper

Skin the tomatoes and chop finely, mix with corned beef. Moisten with sauce and season.

Filling 3:
100 g (4 oz) cream cheese
1 small can pineapple cubes
crush the fruit

Mix ingredients.
Remove crusts from loaves. Slice loaves lengthwise. Make up fillings. Using alternate slices of brown and white, butter the bread and fill with alternate fillings. Sandwich together till desired height is obtained, then cover 'house' with butter.

Coating:
100 g (4 oz) Scottish cheddar
   cheese, grated
25 g (1 oz) cream cheese
salted peanuts or cashew nuts,
   chopped

1 slice gammon (cut into
   tiles)
cucumber
parsley

Coat sides with grated cheese. Pipe cream cheese for windows. Decorate roof with gammon and cucumber. Make a hedge from parsley (see photograph on page 34).

Party Cheese Scones

200 g (8 oz) self raising flour
1 level teaspoon salt
little pepper
1 level teaspoon baking powder
25 g (1 oz) Scottish butter
100 g (4 oz) Scottish cheddar
   cheese, grated
1 egg
125 ml ($\frac{1}{4}$ pint) milk
25 g (1 oz) Scottish cheddar
   cheese, grated, for top

Oven temperature   230°C 450°F Mark 8
Position in oven   Top half
Time in oven   10 minutes

1. Sieve all dry ingredients together then rub in butter.
2. Mix in cheese then add egg and milk. Mix thoroughly to form a fairly soft, light dough.
3. Roll out scone mix into a round 1 cm ($\frac{1}{2}$ inch) thick. Cut into 8 triangles or cut out rounds with a cutter.
4. Sprinkle tops of scones with grated cheese.
5. Place on a floured baking tray and cook in oven until golden brown and firm.

Individual Sponges

100 g (4 oz) Scottish butter
100 g (4 oz) castor sugar
2 eggs
100 g (4 oz) self raising flour,
   sieved

Oven temperature   190°C 375°F Mark 5
Position in oven   Top half
Time in oven   20–25 minutes
Number of servings   16 cakes

1. Lay out 16 paper cases in bun tins.
2. Cream butter and sugar until fluffy then
add an egg and a tablespoon of flour and mix
well. Add second egg in same way then fold in
remaining flour.
3. Place a heaped teaspoon of mixture into
each paper case and bake in oven.
4. Decorate with water icing and write name
with butter icing.

Butter Icing

200 g (8 oz) icing sugar
100 g (4 oz) Scottish butter
2 tablespoons milk
colouring as desired

1. Sieve icing sugar.
2. Cream butter then add icing sugar and
milk alternately.
3. Beat until light and fluffy then add colouring as desired.
4. Use as required.

Peach Ships Ahoy!

1 green jelly
1 medium (439 g or 15½ oz) can
   peach halves
125 ml (¼ pint) fresh double cream
glacé cherries
angelica
wafers

1. Make up jelly as directed on packet.
2. Put aside in cool place to set in shallow
dish.
3. Drain peach halves and place on top of
firm jelly.
4. Decorate with piped cream, cherries and
angelica to make small men.
5. Put half wafers in cream as sails.

Kitten Cake

Sponge:
100 g (4 oz) Scottish butter
100 g (4 oz) castor sugar
150 g (6 oz) self raising flour
2 eggs
1–2 tablespoons hot water

Butter icing:
100 g (4 oz) Scottish butter
200 g (8 oz) icing sugar, sieved
little milk

Decoration:
chocolate vermicelli
desiccated coconut
fruit gums
liquorice
angelica
2 bows

Oven temperature   190°C 375°F Mark 5
Position in oven   Top half
Time in oven   25 minutes

1. Butter two 18 cm (7 inch) round sandwich tins.
2. Make up sponge by creaming butter and sugar together, then add flour and beaten eggs alternately. Finally add a little hot water to give a soft dropping consistency.
3. Place mixture in prepared tins and bake for 25 minutes.
4. Remove from tins and leave to cool.
5. Make up butter icing by creaming butter, then add some icing sugar and a little milk. Beat well then add remainder of icing sugar to give a stiff mixture.
6. Cut sponges as illustrated and stick on ears with butter icing.
7. Cover each sponge completely with butter icing and coat one with vermicelli and one with coconut.
8. Use fruit gums for eyes and nose of each cat.
9. The whiskers for the chocolate cat are six strips of liquorice and the whiskers for the coconut cat are six strips of angelica.
10. Place a bow under each cat's chin.

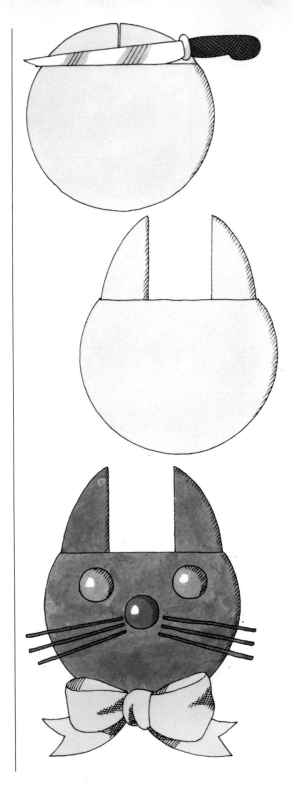

4. Weighty Problems

It is estimated that about half the adult population of this country is overweight to a greater or lesser degree. Excess weight puts great stress on all functions of the body and reduces life expectancy.

People today do not tend to eat too much food but eat the wrong kind of food. When you are trying to reduce weight all the carbohydrate foods e.g. starches and sugars should be avoided, but you must continue to eat milk, cheese, eggs, meat, fish and plenty of fresh fruit and vegetables in order to keep the body in a healthy condition.

If you are greatly overweight the first thing you do before embarking on a slimming diet is to visit your doctor, just to make sure that you are physically fit. If you are only slightly overweight then you may try the slimming diet on the following pages without fear and watch the extra pounds gradually fade away.

In order to obtain the maximum benefit from your slimming diet you must lead an active life. This means moderate exercise and walking as much as possible. The exercises on pages 46, 47, and 48 will also help in conjunction with your diet plan – do them for about 10 minutes three times a day.

Make yourself a weight chart and weigh yourself every day. Do not worry if you do not lose weight some days as the body weight tends to fluctuate. Take more notice of the weekly total – on this diet you should be able to lose up to 3 kg (7 lb) a week.

In an experiment carried out by 15 people who went on this diet the average weight loss over a 4 week period was 5 kg (11 lb). In the first week the average loss was 2½ kg (4½ lb). In the second week the average loss was 1½ kg (3¼ lb), in the third week 1 kg (2¼ lb) and in the fourth week 400 g (1 lb). The people involved in this experiment were of varying age groups and were both men and women.

In this diet you can eat plenty of dairy produce but must cut out carbohydrates. These are foods such as bread, sugar, biscuits, cakes, etc.

The size of portion which you are allowed is as follows:

For a meat portion about 75 g (3 oz)
For a fish portion 125–150 g (5–6 oz)
Chicken on the bone 125–150 g (5–6 oz)

Leafy green vegetables, salads and cauliflowers don't need to be rationed, neither do grapes, oranges, tomatoes or pears. You can drink water when you are thirsty, you can have meat or yeast extracts or a cup of weak tea without sugar or black coffee at any time. One glass of dry wine with dinner if you like or a whiskey and soda or water or a gin and sugar free tonic or dry ginger: no beer or soft drinks or sweet wines please.

If you take sugar in tea or coffee invest in one of the commercial sweeteners and cut out sugar. These sweeteners can be used for cooking and for sweetening fruits like grapefruit. Flour and its products should be cut out and these include cornflour and arrowroot. You can reduce gravies by boiling them rapidly or by adding tomato purée which enriches and thickens a little.

Bad Eating Habits

Many bad eating habits start in childhood and from an early age parents should try to encourage children to eat the right foods. The following points may be helpful:
1. Children need plenty of milk containing calcium to produce healthy bones and teeth.
2. Do not eat between meals.
3. Cut out crisps and biscuits.
4. Ration sweets.
5. Do not fill children up with starchy food.
6. Children should start the day with a good breakfast, with an egg, bacon or one of the breakfasts in the slimming chart.

Foods to Avoid

Sugar
Sweets
Chocolate
Alcohol and sweet soft drinks
Cakes
Pies
Pastry
Biscuits
Heavy puddings
Honey
Syrup
Treacle
Jam
Crisps
Nuts
Too many potatoes
Spaghetti
Macaroni and other pasta
Too much bread and cereal
Bananas
Too many fried foods
   If you feel hungry drink a glass of milk and eat an apple.

One Week's Menu

On the following pages, you will find suggestions for a complete week's meals designed for those who want a healthy, balanced diet —and who want to loose some weight.

	Early Tea	Breakfast	Mid Morning
Monday	Early morning tea (no sugar or biscuits)	Fresh fruit juice (no sugar) Boiled egg 1 thin slice bread, buttered Tea or coffee (no sugar)	Tea or coffee (no sugar) or Yeast or meat extract or Pear or orange
Tuesday	Early morning tea (no sugar or biscuits) or Fresh fruit juice	Half a grapefruit (no sugar) Smoked haddock in butter Tea or coffee	one of above
Wednesday	Early morning tea (no sugar or biscuits) or Fresh fruit juice	Unsweetened juice 2 egg omelette with parsley or tomato Tea or coffee (no sugar)	one of above
Thursday	Early morning tea (no sugar or biscuits) or Fresh fruit juice	Fresh orange Kipper fillet in butter Tea or coffee (no sugar)	one of above
Friday	Early morning tea (no sugar or biscuits) or Fresh fruit juice	Half a grapefruit (no sugar) Large bowl of Branflakes 1 teaspoon cream and plenty of milk or Oatmeal porridge with cream Tea or coffee (no sugar)	one of above
Saturday	Early morning tea (no sugar or biscuits) or Fresh fruit juice	Fresh fruit juice 1 egg and 2 rashers bacon Tea or coffee (no sugar)	one of above
Sunday	Early morning tea (no sugar or biscuits) or Fresh fruit juice	Scrambled egg 1 rasher bacon 1 grilled tomato Tea or coffee (no sugar)	one of above

Main Meal	Other Meal	Tea Break	Supper
Clear unthickened soup or melon or tomato juice Roast, casseroled or grilled meat with unthickened gravy Green vegetables and butter Fresh fruit and cream or stewed fruit and yogurt	Small cheese salad – 50 g (2 oz) cheese, lettuce tomato, cucumber. Add little oil and vinegar if desired Glass of milk	Tea (no sugar)	Cup of Milk (hot or cold)
Clear soup or melon or tomato juice Chicken or duck, roasted, grilled or fried (no batter – thickened gravy allowed) Fresh fruit or real egg custard served with sliced oranges	Toasted cheese 50 g (2 oz) cheese on 1 thin slice of bread Glass of milk	Tea (no sugar)	Cup of milk (hot or cold)
Clear soup or tomato juice Fillet of steak or fish, grilled or baked 1 tablespoon potato, mashed with milk and butter	50 g (2 oz) any cheese with 1 piece thin bread or crisp bread, buttered Tomato or celery Glass of milk	Tea (no sugar)	Cup of milk (hot or cold)
Cream of cauliflower soup, with cream added Mixed grill of lamb cutlet, piece liver and finger of rump steak, mushroom, tomato and green vegetable Fresh fruit salad and cream	2 tomatoes stuffed with 50 g (2 oz) grated cheese and a little cream or mayonnaise 1 thin slice toast or crisp bread, buttered Glass of milk	Tea (no sugar)	Cup of milk (hot or cold)
Clear soup or fresh juice Roast lamb or beef with unthickened gravy Half packet crisps, heated Green vegetable Fresh fruit salad with cream	Sole à la Crème (page 55) Glass of milk 1 thin slice bread, buttered	Tea (no sugar)	Cup of milk (hot or cold)
French onion soup with grated cheese or beef broth Shepherd's pie made with sliced tomato and beaten egg and milk instead of potato Green vegetable Milk jelly and fresh fruit	A good helping cottage cheese, lettuce, tomato, and watercress Glass of milk	Tea (no sugar)	Cup of milk (hot or cold)
Clear soup or unsweetened grapefruit Baked fish with tomato and green vegetables Stewed fruit sweetened with a sweetener and baked custard or cream	1 thin slice bread, buttered 50 g (2 oz) any cheese you like, pickled onion and a tomato Glass of milk	Tea (no sugar)	Cup of milk (hot or cold)

Weight Graph

To encourage you to keep to your diet and to enable you to watch the pounds slip off, use the graph on the opposite page.

Put your starting weight in the appropriate place at the top of the graph and each day fill in your weight and watch the graph curve down as your weight reduces. If you are starting at 11 st 9 lb, and you lose 1 lb each day for a week, the top of your graph would start like this (below).

Fill in the appropriate stones weight where they are relevant to you. For a person who is 11 st 9 lb, the graph at the top should read 12 stone, and the graph reading down should be 11 st 13 lb etc. to 11 st, and so on to the foot of the graph which will go down to 8 st.

For a person who is 15 st 3 lb, the graph at the top should start at 16 st.

If you are being weighed in kilogrammes, there is a conversion table below to help you.

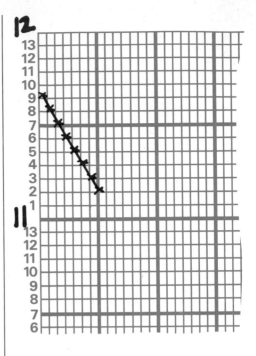

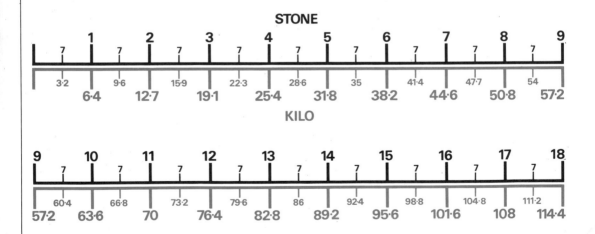

44

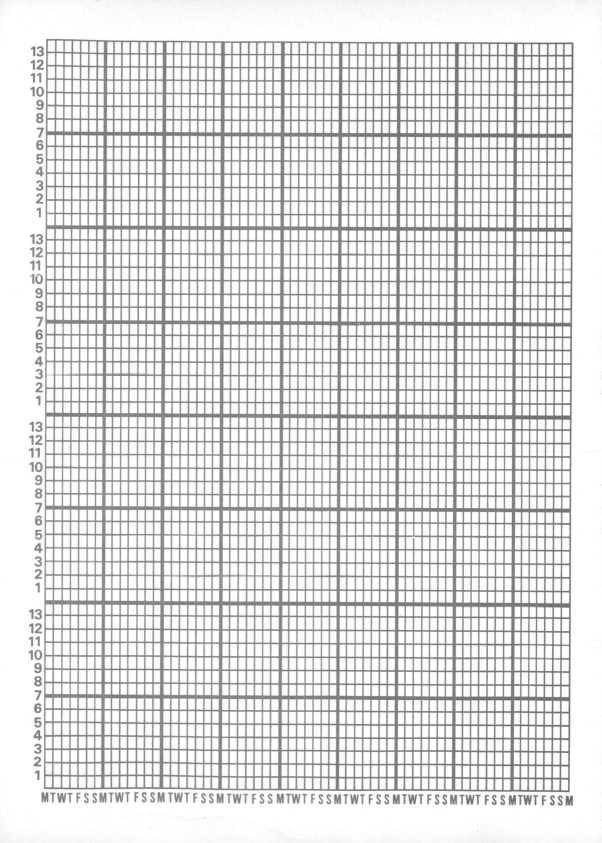

Slimming Exercises

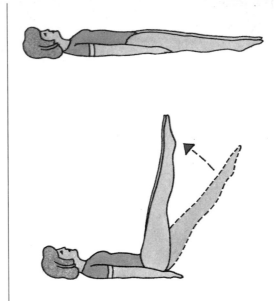

Exercise 1

1. Stand erect, feet together, arms out-stretched, shoulders back, head up.
2. Keeping back straight and head up, bring arms back to hips and bend knees. Stand erect.

Exercise 3

1. Lie on floor on your back with arms at your side, legs straight out. Relax.
2. Keeping legs together, lift them in the air until they are at right angles to your body. Keep head and back on floor all the time. Relax slowly, lowering legs, still together, until they are straight out on the floor.

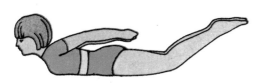

Exercise 2

1. Lie face down on the floor, arms behind back, hands held loosely together. Relax.
2. Stretch arms and lift legs and head at same time. Relax.

Exercise 4

From the starting position for Exercise Three, raise legs again, but this time swing them right over your head until your toes touch the floor behind your head. Keep your hands at your side.

Exercise 5

1. Lie on floor, legs together in the air, hands supporting hips, and feet pointing to the ceiling.
2. Move hands from hips, and place them flat on the floor. At the same time start pedalling in the air with your legs.

Exercise 7

Stand erect, head up, shoulders back, legs apart. Bend arms, hands on shoulders. Pull elbows back as far as possible. Relax and repeat.

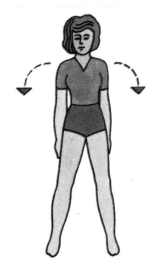

Exercise 6

1. Lie on the floor with your knees drawn up to your chest, hands clasped around your knees.
2. Keeping tightly rolled, rock from side to side.

Exercise 8

Stand erect, feet apart and arms at your side. Slowly bend from side to side.

Exercise 9

Lie face down on floor, arms at your side. Raise one leg at a time slowly, keeping knees straight. Repeat, raising both legs together.

Exercise 11

1. Lie on floor on back with arms at your side, legs straight out.
2. Slowly raise one leg at a time, keeping knees straight.
3. Repeat, raising both legs together and keeping knees straight.

Exercise 10

1. Lie on floor on back with knees bent up and feet flat on floor. Stretch arms out on floor above head.
2. Slowly bring right hand down to touch left knee. Repeat, bringing left hand down to touch right knee.

5. Dairy Recipes

The recipes in this chapter are a mixture of personal favourites and brand new recipes made up especially for this book. There are a few recipes for dinner parties or special occasions, but the majority are for everyday use and are very simple and straightforward to make. You will be able to give your family a whole range of appetising, nutritious meals knowing that every one has the goodness of dairy produce in some form or another.

French Onion Soup

300 g (12 oz) onions, sliced thinly
37 g (1½ oz) Scottish butter
salt and pepper
750 ml (1¼ pints) beef stock
¼ teaspoon gravy browning
1 or 2 tablespoons dry sherry
  (optional)
2 slices toasted cheese

Number of servings 4

1. Fry onions gently in butter until golden brown in colour – about 15 minutes. Season, add stock and browning, bring to boil then reduce heat and simmer for 45 minutes.
2. Season and add sherry.
3. Serve garnished with diced toasted cheese.

Cream of Mushroom Soup

150 g (6 oz) mushrooms, washed
  and sliced
50 g (2 oz) Scottish butter
25 g (1 oz) plain flour
750 ml (1¼ pints) stock or
  2 chicken stock cubes made up
  to 750 ml (1¼ pints)
250 ml (½ pint) milk
salt and pepper
3–4 tablespoons fresh cream

Number of servings 4

1. Fry mushrooms in butter for 5 minutes.
2. Add flour and cook for a further 5 minutes, stirring occasionally.
3. Gradually add stock and bring to boil, stirring all the time.
4. Simmer for ½ hour then add milk.
5. Test for seasoning.
6. When serving add a little cream to the centre of soup in plate.

Photograph shows French *Onion Soup, Cheese and Onion Soup, Cream of Mushroom Soup.

Cheese and Onion Soup

1 large onion, finely chopped
25 g (1 oz) Scottish butter
25 g (1 oz) plain flour
1 level teaspoon dry mustard
500 ml (1 pint) milk
125 ml (¼ pint) chicken stock
salt and pepper
100 g (4 oz) Scottish cheddar
  cheese, finely grated
1 tablespoon chopped parsley

Number of servings 4

1. Fry onion gently in butter until soft but not brown.
2. Stir in flour and mustard. Cook slowly for 2 minutes. Remove pan from heat, gradually blend in milk and stock.
3. Return to heat, cook, stirring, until soup comes to boil and thickens slightly.
4. Season to taste with salt and pepper. Lower heat and cover pan.
5. Simmer very gently for 15 minutes.
6. Remove from heat. Add cheese, stir until melted.
7. Pour soup into soup tureen and sprinkle with chopped parsley.

Cream of Corn Soup

1 rasher bacon, chopped
1 small onion, finely chopped
25 g (1 oz) Scottish butter
2 large potatoes, sliced
1 stalk celery
250 ml ($\frac{1}{2}$ pint) chicken stock
salt and pepper
1 small (175 g or 7 oz) can corn
   kernels
1–2 teaspoons cornflour
500 ml (1 pint) milk

Number of servings   5–6

1. Fry bacon and onion in butter till clear then add potato and celery.
2. Add stock and seasoning and simmer till potatoes and other vegetables are soft. Add the corn.
3. Blend cornflour with a little milk and add it to rest of milk. Add this to the corn mixture and bring to boiling point and simmer for 5 minutes.
4. Sieve the soup or put in an electric blender.
5. Serve with croûtons.

Creamed Potato and Leek Soup

5 leeks, washed and sliced
25 g (1 oz) Scottish butter
5 medium potatoes, roughly diced
500 ml (1 pint) water
salt and pepper
625 ml (1$\frac{1}{4}$ pints) milk
2 egg yolks
125 ml ($\frac{1}{4}$ pint) fresh single cream
1 tablespoon chopped parsley

Number of servings   4–6

1. Sauté leeks in butter until soft. Add potatoes, water, salt and pepper.
2. Bring to boil, reduce heat and simmer for 45 minutes. Sieve or liquidise mixture and add milk. Bring to boiling point and cook for 5 minutes.
3. Blend egg yolks carefully with cream.
4. Stir in a little of the hot soup and return mixture to the pan.
5. Cook very gently for 5 minutes, stirring frequently. Season to taste and garnish with chopped parsley.

Prawn Cocktail

1 lettuce heart
200 g (8 oz) prawns
125 ml (¼ pint) fresh double cream
2 tablespoons mayonnaise
little lemon juice
tomato ketchup to colour
salt and pepper
4 lemon slices
paprika

Number of servings   4

1. Wash and shred lettuce and place in the base of 4 glasses.
2. Divide the prawns between the 4 glasses retaining 4 to garnish.
3. Make up dressing by whipping cream lightly then mix in mayonnaise, lemon juice and sufficient tomato ketchup to colour pale pink. Season to taste.
4. Pour dressing over prawns and garnish with a slice of lemon, a prawn and a little paprika.
5. Serve with fingers of buttered brown bread.

Peach Delight

4 peach halves
4 lettuce leaves
50 g (2 oz) shrimps or prawns
100 g (4 oz) Scottish cheddar
    cheese, grated
1–2 tablespoons fresh double
    cream, lightly whipped
1–2 tablespoons salad cream
salt and pepper
4 slices cucumber

Number of servings   4

1. Drain peach halves and place each on a lettuce leaf.
2. Mix shrimps and cheese and bind together with lightly whipped cream and salad cream. Season to taste.
3. Pile mixture on top of each peach and garnish with a twist of cucumber.

Herbie Haddock

3 fillets haddock
salt and pepper
25 g (1 oz) Scottish butter
2 tablespoons breadcrumbs
$\frac{1}{2}$ teaspoon mixed dried herbs
3 tablespoons Scottish cheddar
  cheese, grated
little milk

Oven temperature   190°C 375°F Mark 5
Position in oven   Centre
Time in oven   15–20 minutes
Number of servings   3

1. Wash fish, season and place in an oven-proof dish.
2. Melt butter and add breadcrumbs, herbs and grated cheese, mix well.
3. Place some of the mixture on top of each fillet then pour a little milk round the fish.
4. Bake in a moderate oven.
5. When cooked, brown under grill to crisp up topping.

Sole à la Crème

75 g (3 oz) Scottish butter
4 fillets lemon sole
juice of one lemon
100 g (4 oz) fresh double cream
salt and pepper

Number of servings   4

1. Melt butter in frying pan and gently fry sole in butter with lemon juice added. When sole is cooked, remove it from pan and keep warm.
2. Add cream to butter and lemon juice, and bring to boil. Boil for 1 to 2 minutes, until all ingredients are mixed together and begin to thicken.
3. Test for seasoning. Remove from heat immediately and pour over sole.

Photograph shows Herbie Haddock, Sole à la Crème, Haddock Farci (page 56).

Russian Fish Pie

2 small fillets haddock
1 (187 g or 7$\frac{1}{2}$ oz) packet puff
  pastry
25 g (1 oz) Scottish butter
25 g (1 oz) plain flour
170 ml ($\frac{1}{3}$ pint) milk
50 g (2 oz) Scottish cheddar
  cheese, grated
salt and pepper

Oven temperature   220°C 425°F Mark 7
Position in oven   Top half
Time in oven   25–30 minutes
Number of servings   4

1. Cook fish in a little milk, strain and flake.
2. Roll out pastry into 2 squares.
3. Melt butter, remove from heat, add flour, and slowly blend in milk. Bring to the boil, stirring all the time. Add grated cheese and fish, season to taste.
4. Use mixture to spread on bottom layer of pastry. Wet edges, lay on 2nd square of pastry and seal.
5. Brush with milk and bake in preheated oven till golden brown.

Haddock Cheddar Pie

200 g (8 oz) filleted haddock
250 ml (½ pint) milk
25 g (1 oz) Scottish butter
25 g (1 oz) plain flour
100 g (4 oz) Scottish cheddar
  cheese, grated
salt and pepper
little mustard
400 g (1 lb) mashed potato
parsley

Oven temperature   180°C 350°F Mark 4
Position in oven   Centre
Time in oven   10–15 minutes
Number of servings   4

1. Poach fish gently in milk, remove from milk and flake. Reserve milk for sauce.
2. Melt butter in pan, add flour then gradually add milk. Bring to boil, stirring all the time. Add most of cheese, salt and pepper and mustard, then the flaked fish.
3. Place mixture in an ovenproof dish and pipe potatoes on top. Sprinkle remainder of cheese on top.
4. Place in oven until golden brown. Garnish with parsley.

Haddock Farci

Stuffing:
100 g (4 oz) Scottish cheddar
  cheese, grated
50 g (2 oz) fresh breadcrumbs
1 tablespoon chopped parsley
salt and pepper
1 egg

4 pieces filleted haddock
salt, pepper and lemon juice
seasoned flour
37 g (1½ oz) Scottish butter
1 egg and breadcrumbs for coating
parsley and lemon slices to
  garnish

Oven temperature   200°C 400°F Mark 6
Position in oven   Top half
Time in oven   20–25 minutes
Number of servings   4

1. Make up stuffing by mixing cheese, breadcrumbs, parsley and seasoning, then bind together with egg.
2. Sprinkle fillets with seasoning and lemon juice, then dust with seasoned flour.
3. Divide stuffing into four and roll up stuffing in each fillet.
4. Coat fillets with egg and breadcrumbs.
5. Melt butter in a baking tin in the oven and when hot, place fillets in butter and baste well. Bake in a fairly hot oven for 20–25 minutes.
6. Serve garnished with parsley and lemon.

Cheese, Mushroom and Tuna Bake

1 small (99 g or 3½ oz) can tuna fish
200 g (8 oz) mushrooms
100 g (4 oz) Scottish cheddar
   cheese, grated
1 tablespoon white breadcrumbs
salt and pepper
3 tablespoons top of the milk

Oven temperature   165°C 325°F Mark 3
Position in oven   Top of oven
Time in oven   25 minutes (approx.)
Number of servings   2–3

1. Strain and flake the tuna fish and put into a greased ovenproof dish.
2. Slice the mushrooms thinly, and place on top of fish.
3. Mix the grated cheese, breadcrumbs and seasoning together.
4. Sprinkle over mushrooms.
5. Pour milk over the mixture, and put in oven for about 25 minutes until top is brown and crisp.

Haddock Surprise

300 g (12 oz) smoked haddock
salt and pepper
100 g (4 oz) Scottish butter,
   softened
6 eggs, hardboiled and chopped
250 ml (½ pint) fresh double cream
100 g (4 oz) Scottish cheddar
   cheese, grated
1 tomato, sliced
parsley to garnish

Number of servings   4

1. Place the haddock in a pan with a little water and some salt and pepper.
2. Cover and simmer over a low heat for 15 minutes to poach the fish.
3. When cooked, drain the fish, flake it and mix with the butter, eggs and cream.
4. Place in an ovenproof dish, sprinkle with the cheese and top with tomato slices.
5. Place under a hot grill until the top is golden brown.
6. Serve sprinkled with chopped parsley.

Favourite Fish Pie

400 g (1 lb) haddock
250 ml (½ pint) milk
25 g (1 oz) Scottish butter
25 g (1 oz) plain flour
50 g (2 oz) shrimps
salt and pepper
400 g (1 lb) potatoes, mashed
50 g (2 oz) Scottish cheddar
   cheese, grated

Oven temperature   220°C 425°F Mark 7
Position in oven   Top half
Time in oven   15 minutes
Number of servings   4

1. Poach haddock in milk then use milk for sauce. Flake fish.
2. To make the sauce melt the butter, and blend in the flour. Gradually add milk retained from cooking the fish.
3. Bring to the boil, stirring all the time and cook for 2–3 minutes.
4. Add shrimps, flaked fish and seasoning. Mix well and place in ovenproof dish.
5. Pipe or spread potatoes on top and sprinkle with cheese.
6. Bake for 15 minutes.

Beef Stroganoff

600 g (1½ lb) rump steak
1 small onion, grated
75 g (3 oz) Scottish butter
300 g (12 oz) button mushrooms,
    sliced
salt and pepper
3 tablespoons white wine
125 ml (¼ pint) fresh double cream
1 green and 1 red pepper, sliced
Accompaniments:
300 g (12 oz) rice or noodles

Number of servings   6

1. Beat steak with rolling pin and cut into
1 cm (½ inch) wide strips. Fry onion in half of
butter for 5 minutes, add steak strips and fry
for a further 10 minutes, turning all the time.
2. Add rest of butter and mushrooms, cook
for 3 minutes. Season to taste.
3. Gradually stir in wine and cook for a
further 5 minutes or until meat is tender.
4. Add cream just before serving. Serve on a
bed of rice or noodles and garnish with red
and green peppers.
N.B. Cook rice by boiling in a large pan of
salted water for 12–15 minutes. Strain and
rinse with boiling water. Drain thoroughly,
place in serving dish and dry off in a moderate
oven for 10 minutes.

Photograph shows Beef Stroganoff, Cidered
Pork Fillets, Soured Cream Pork.

Cidered Pork Fillets

2 pork fillets
1 onion, sliced
50 g (2 oz) Scottish butter
100 g (4 oz) mushrooms, sliced
25 g (1 oz) plain flour
125 ml (¼ pint) cider
salt and pepper
75 ml (⅛ pint) fresh double cream

Number of servings   5–6

1. Cut pork fillets into cubes.
2. Fry onion and pork in butter for 5 minutes.
Add mushrooms and cook for further 5
minutes. Add flour and stir in thoroughly.
3. Gradually add cider, stirring all the time.
Stew for 25 minutes, season to taste.
4. Just before serving add the cream.

Soured Cream Pork

400 g (1 lb) pork fillet or
    tenderloin
seasoned flour
50 g (2 oz) Scottish butter
100 g (4 oz) streaky bacon,
    chopped
1 medium (326 g or 11½ oz) can
    sweet corn
200 g (8 oz) tomato chutney
125 ml (¼ pint) fresh double cream
1 tablespoon lemon juice
salt and pepper

Number of servings   4–5

1. Cut pork into strips and coat well in
seasoned flour. Heat butter in pan and fry
pork until lightly brown, turning frequently.
Remove from pan.
2. Fry bacon until crisp. Add sweet corn and
tomato chutney and simmer for 2–3 minutes.
3. Sour the cream by mixing with the lemon
juice.
4. Return pork to pan, add cream and
lemon juice, stir well and bring to boil.
5. Check for seasoning and simmer gently
for about 20 minutes stirring occasionally.
6. Serve with diced fried potatoes.

59

Sirloin Steaks and Parsley Butter

Parsley butter:
50 g (2 oz) Scottish butter
1 tablespoon chopped parsley
little lemon juice
salt and pepper

4 sirloin steaks
little Scottish butter
salt and pepper

Number of servings 4

1. Make up parsley butter by creaming butter well, then add parsley, lemon juice and seasoning. Wrap this up in greaseproof paper in the form of a long roll and place in refrigerator until required.
2. Beat steaks, brush with melted butter and season.
3. Pre-heat grill and grill steaks on both sides for 3–7 minutes, according to taste.
4. Serve steaks garnished with parsley butter accompanied by a green salad.

Sussex Chicken

2 chicken portions
salt and pepper
1 packet crisps
50 g (2 oz) Scottish cheddar
   cheese, grated
50 g (2 oz) Scottish butter

Oven temperature 190°C 375°F Mark 5
Position in oven Centre
Time in oven 30–35 minutes
Number of servings 2

1. Skin and season the chicken portions.
2. Crush the crisps and mix with cheese.
3. Melt butter and dip chicken portions in this, then into crisp and cheese mixture giving chicken a good coating.
4. Arrange portions in an ovenproof dish and pour remainder of butter over chicken.
5. Bake, uncovered, in middle of a fairly hot oven for 30–35 minutes.

Savoury Meringue Nests

50 g (2 oz) bacon, chopped
100 g (4 oz) mushrooms, chopped
25 g (1 oz) Scottish butter
600 g (1½ lb) potatoes, mashed or
   3 serving packet potato mix
1 egg, separated
salt and pepper
100 g (4 oz) Scottish cheddar
   cheese (½ finely grated,
   ½ coarsely grated)
parsley

Oven temperature 190°C 375°F Mark 5
Position in oven Centre
Time in oven 15 minutes
Number of servings 4

1. Sauté bacon and mushrooms together in butter for 5 minutes.
2. Make up potatoes and mix with egg yolk and seasoning.
3. Pipe potato into nest shapes on greased baking sheet.
4. Mix cooked bacon with mushrooms and coarsely grated cheese, fill nests with mixture.
5. Whisk egg white till stiff, season and fold in most of the finely grated cheese. Pile on top of nests and sprinkle remaining cheese on top.
6. Place in oven for 15 minutes. Garnish with parsley.

Baked Tomatoes with Corn

3 tomatoes
½ small (198 g or 7 oz) can corn
   kernels
2 tablespoons fresh cream
salt and pepper

Oven temperature 180°C 350°F Mark 4
Position in oven Centre
Time in oven 10 minutes
Number of servings 3

1. Halve tomatoes and scoop out pulp.
2. Mix pulp with corn, cream and seasoning.
3. Fill up halves of tomato with mixture.
4. Bake in oven for 10 minutes.

Chicken Supreme

1 boiling fowl, cooked
50 g (2 oz) Scottish butter
1 tablespoon chopped onion
50 g (2 oz) plain flour
500 ml (1 pint) milk
1 small packet frozen peas,
  cooked
1 small packet frozen sweet corn,
  cooked
salt and pepper to taste
1 tablespoon fresh double or
  single cream
1½ cups long grain rice
generous litre (2 pints) water
1 chicken stock cube

Number of servings   6–8

1. Remove meat from chicken and chop roughly.
2. Melt butter in saucepan, add onion and cook gently for 5 minutes, stirring occasionally, then add flour.
3. Gradually blend in milk and bring to the boil stirring all the time, boil for a few minutes.
4. Add chicken, peas and sweet corn to sauce and mix well. Season to taste and stir in cream.
5. Boil rice in water with stock cube added for 12 minutes, drain and serve round the outside of a platter.
6. Arrange chicken mixture in the centre of the rice.
7. Garnish with parsley.

Oriental Medley

75 g (3 oz) Scottish butter
200 g (8 oz) long grain rice
1 chicken stock cube
750 ml (1½ pints) boiling water
3 tomatoes, skinned and chopped
100 g (4 oz) mushrooms, sliced
  and fried
1 medium onion, sliced
100 g (4 oz) bacon, fried and
  chopped
150 g (6 oz) cooked chicken, diced
50 g (2 oz) Scottish cheddar
  cheese, grated
tomatoes and parsley to garnish

Number of servings   4

1. Melt butter in frying pan and fry rice till golden brown.
2. Dissolve stock cube in boiling water and stir into rice.
3. Simmer until liquid has evaporated, about 10–15 minutes.
4. Add tomatoes, mushrooms, onion, bacon and chicken and heat thoroughly.
5. Just before serving mix grated cheese through and serve garnished with tomato and parsley.

Italian Stuffed Pancakes

Filling:
200 g (8 oz) streaky bacon
2 medium onions, chopped
2 tablespoons oil
100 g (4 oz) mushrooms, peeled
  and sliced
1 medium (226 g or 8 oz) can
  tomatoes
salt and pepper

Batter:
100 g (4 oz) plain flour
pinch of salt
1 egg
250 ml (½ pint) milk

Parmesan cheese to garnish
Scottish butter for frying

Number of servings   5–6

Filling:
1. Remove rind from bacon and chop.
2. Fry bacon and onions in oil for 5 minutes.
Add mushrooms and cook for a further 2–3
minutes.
3. Stir in tomatoes and add salt and pepper.
Bring to the boil. Reduce to simmering point
for 10 minutes. Keep warm.
Batter:
4. Sieve flour and salt into bowl. Make a well
in the centre.
5. Drop the egg into the well, add half of the
milk and begin mixing, gradually drawing
the flour into the liquid. Beat well then
lightly beat in the rest of the milk.
6. Fry the pancakes then pile them on a hot
dish with a piece of buttered foil between each
pancake. Keep them hot in the oven.
7. Divide the filling between the pancakes
reserving a little for garnish.
8. Roll up pancakes, arrange on dish. Pour
over remaining filling and sprinkle with
Parmesan cheese. Serve.

Photograph shows Italian Stuffed Pancakes,
Pizza Pie, Noodle Nest (page 64).

Pizza Pie

100 g (4 oz) plain flour
4 level teaspoons baking powder
salt and pepper
pinch mixed herbs
3–4 tablespoons water to mix
50 g (2 oz) Scottish butter (for frying)

Filling:
4 tomatoes, skinned and chopped
  roughly
150 g (6 oz) Scottish cheddar
  cheese, grated
salt and pepper

anchovy fillets and parsley to
  garnish

Number of servings   6

1. Sieve flour, baking powder, salt and pepper
into a bowl. Add a pinch of mixed herbs and
enough water to mix to an elastic dough.
2. Roll out and shape into a circle to fit your
frying pan about 18 cm (7 inches).
3. Melt butter in pan and fry pizza dough
until golden brown on one side. Turn over
and place tomatoes and cheese on cooked
side, season.
4. Cover frying pan with a tight fitting lid
and cook slowly until cheese melts. Garnish
with anchovy fillets and parsley.

Lasagne with Yogurt Topping

Meat sauce:
12 g (½ oz) lard
1 medium onion, chopped
400 g (1 lb) lean minced beef
1 level teaspoon dried mixed
   herbs
1 medium (226 g or 8 oz) can
   peeled tomatoes
salt and pepper
2 level teaspoons cornflour
1 tablespoon Worcestershire
   sauce

Cheese sauce:
25 g (1 oz) Scottish butter
25 g (1 oz) plain flour
250 ml (½ pint) milk
¼ level teaspoon dry mustard
37 g (1½ oz) Scottish cheddar
   cheese, grated
salt and pepper

6 sheets lasagne (100 g or 4 oz)

Yogurt topping:
1 carton (125 g or 5 oz) natural
   yogurt
1 egg, beaten
12 g (½ oz) plain flour
2 tomatoes, sliced

Oven temperature   190°C 375°F Mark 5
Position in oven   Centre
Time in oven   25 minutes
Number of servings   4

1. Preheat oven.
2. Melt lard in a pan and gently fry onion for 3 minutes, until soft.
3. Add beef, herbs and tomatoes and bring to the boil, stirring. Season to taste.
4. Simmer, uncovered, for 30 minutes.
5. Mix cornflour with Worcestershire sauce and stir into the meat.
6. Return to the boil for 1 minute, stirring.
7. To make cheese sauce, melt butter in a pan, stir in flour off the heat and blend in milk. Return to heat and bring to boil, stirring.
8. Remove from heat. Add mustard, cheese and seasoning.
9. Cook pasta: place in boiling salted water for 11 minutes, drain.
10. To make up the dish, arrange the meat, lasagne and cheese sauce in layers, in a 1½ litre (3 pint) ovenproof dish, finishing with layer of lasagne.
11. To make topping, whisk yogurt, egg and flour together and spoon over lasagne. Decorate with sliced tomatoes. Bake in the centre of the oven for 20–25 minutes, until topping is set.

Noodle Nest

150 g (6 oz) flat noodles

Basic coating sauce:
25 g (1 oz) Scottish butter
25 g (1 oz) plain flour
250 ml (½ pint) milk

200 g (8 oz) Scottish cheddar
   cheese, finely grated
200 g (8 oz) carrots, sliced and
   cooked
200 g (8 oz) peas, cooked
salt and pepper
4 eggs, hardboiled
chopped parsley

Number of servings   4

1. Cook noodles in boiling salted water until tender (20 minutes), or according to packet directions.
2. Drain and arrange in ring on a warm dish. Keep hot.
3. Make basic coating sauce, by melting butter, adding flour, then slowly adding milk. Bring to boil, stirring, then add 150 g (6 oz) of the cheese. Add carrots and peas. Season to taste.
4. Halve the hardboiled eggs.
5. Pour sauce mixture into noodle ring. Arrange hardboiled eggs on top.
6. Sprinkle with the remaining cheese mixed with some chopped parsley. Serve at once.

Savoury Quiche

Cheese pastry:
50 g (2 oz) Scottish butter
100 g (4 oz) plain flour, sieved
salt, pepper, mustard
25 g (1 oz) Scottish cheddar
cheese, grated

Filling:
4 rashers bacon, sliced
100 g (4 oz) mushrooms, sliced
100 g (4 oz) Scottish cheddar
cheese, grated
2 eggs
250 ml (½ pint) milk
salt, pepper, mustard

Oven temperature   220°C 425°F Mark 7
                   190°C 375°F Mark 5
Position in oven   Top half
Time in oven   30 minutes
Number of servings   4–6

1. Make up pastry in usual way by rubbing butter into flour. Add seasoning and grated cheese then add sufficient water to make into a stiff dough.
2. Roll out pastry and line an 18 cm (7 inch) flan ring or sandwich tin.
3. Bake 'blind' in a fairly hot oven for about 20 minutes. Fry bacon and mushrooms, slice and arrange in pastry case.
4. Cover with grated cheese. Beat eggs, add milk and seasoning and pour into flan.
5. Bake in hot oven for 10 minutes then reduce heat to 190°C (375°F) for 15–20 minutes till set. Serve hot or cold.

Risotto

100 g (4 oz) long grain rice
1 chicken stock cube
750 ml (1½ pints) water
100 g (4 oz) mushrooms, peeled
and sliced
1 small onion, chopped
75 g (3 oz) Scottish butter
4 tomatoes, skinned and sliced
1 portion chicken, cooked and
chopped
salt and pepper
50 g (2 oz) Scottish cheddar
cheese

Number of servings   4

1. Boil rice in chicken stock cube and water for 12 minutes, drain well.
2. Fry mushrooms and onion in butter until cooked.
3. Add tomatoes, chopped chicken and rice.
4. Season and put in an ovenproof dish, sprinkle grated cheese on top and brown lightly under the grill.

Cheese Pudding

50 g (2 oz) breadcrumbs
250 ml (½ pint) milk
75 g (3 oz) Scottish cheddar
cheese, grated
25 g (1 oz) Scottish butter
1 egg, separated
salt and pepper

Oven temperature   190°C 375°F Mark 5
Position in oven   Centre
Time in oven   35 minutes
Number of servings   3–4

1. Put breadcrumbs into a basin and pour on boiling milk. Leave to stand for 10 minutes.
2. Add cheese, butter, egg yolk and seasoning.
3. Beat the egg white stiffly and fold into the mixture.
4. Pour into a greased, 1 litre (1½ pint) ovenproof dish and bake till set.
5. Serve immediately.

Cheese Curry

100 g (4 oz) long grain rice
salt
25 g (1 oz) Scottish butter
1 onion, chopped
25 g (1 oz) plain flour
2–3 teaspoons curry powder
250 ml ($\frac{1}{2}$ pint) water
25 g (1 oz) sultanas
1 apple, chopped
200 g (8 oz) Scottish cheddar
   cheese, grated
1 tomato, diced

Number of servings   3–4

1. Cook rice in boiling salted water until just soft – about 12 minutes.
2. Drain rice, rinse with boiling water and dry on a baking tray either in a warm oven or under a low grill.
3. Melt butter in saucepan and fry onion until golden.
4. Add flour and curry powder and stir over a gentle heat.
5. Add water gradually, stirring thoroughly until sauce thickens.
6. Add sultanas and chopped apple and cook for a few minutes.
7. Stir in the cheese.
8. Garnish curry with diced tomato and serve with the rice.

Ham, Cheese and Mushroom Risotto

100 g (4 oz) Scottish butter
1 medium onion, thinly sliced
150 g (6 oz) long grain rice
500 ml (1 pint) hot chicken stock
2 tomatoes, skinned and chopped
salt and pepper
100 g (4 oz) mushrooms, sliced and
   fried
100 g (4 oz) ham, sliced and fried
200 g (8 oz) Scottish cheddar
   cheese, diced

Number of servings   4

1. Melt butter in saucepan and fry onion lightly.
2. Add rice and cook for a few minutes.
3. Add stock, tomatoes and seasoning. Bring to boil.
4. Cover and simmer gently until all stock has been absorbed, stirring occasionally (about 20–25 minutes).
5. During this time cook mushrooms and ham, dice cheese.
6. Mix in cooked ham and mushrooms and cheese quickly.
Serve at once in a hot serving dish.

Cheese and Parsley Soufflé

25g (1 oz) Scottish butter
25 g (1 oz) plain flour
170 ml ($\frac{1}{3}$ pint) milk
75 g (3 oz) Scottish cheddar
   cheese, grated
1 tablespoon parsley, chopped
salt and pepper
3 eggs, separated

Oven temperature 220°C 425°F Mark 7
Position in oven Centre
Time in oven 30 minutes
Number of servings 3–4

1. Butter a 1 litre (1$\frac{1}{2}$ pint) soufflé or oven-proof dish.
2. Melt butter in pan, stir in flour, gradually add milk and bring sauce to boil, stirring all the time.
3. Add cheese, parsley, seasoning and egg yolks, beat well.
4. Whisk egg whites until stiff and fold them into sauce mixture.
5. Pour mixture into prepared dish and bake in over for about 30 minutes. Serve immediately.

Cheesy Sausage Pie

600 g (1$\frac{1}{2}$ lb) potatoes
200 g (8 oz) Scottish cheddar
   cheese, grated
400 g (1 lb) link sausages
4 tomatoes, skinned

Oven temperature 220°C 425°F Mark 7
Position in oven Centre
Time in oven 10 minutes
Number of servings 4

1. Boil potatoes for 20–25 minutes, drain and mash. Add cheese and mix well.
2. Grill sausages for 15 minutes.
3. Arrange sausages and sliced tomatoes alternately in base of 1$\frac{1}{2}$–2 litre (2$\frac{1}{2}$–3 pint) ovenproof dish.
4. Spread or pipe cheesy potato over sausages and tomatoes.
5. Bake till lightly brown.

Crunchy Cheese Flan

Cheese pastry:
50 g (2 oz) Scottish butter
100 g (4 oz) plain flour
50 g (2 oz) Scottish cheddar
   cheese, grated
salt, pepper, mustard
about 1 tablespoon cold water

Filling:
150 g (6 oz) Scottish cheddar
   cheese, coarsely grated
3 rashers bacon, cooked and
   chopped
2 egg yolks
salt and pepper
6 tablespoons milk

Topping:
2 egg whites
50 g (2 oz) Scottish cheddar
   cheese, finely grated
salt and pepper

Oven temperature 190°C 375°F Mark 5
                    150°C 300°F Mark 2
Position in oven Centre
Time in oven 20 minutes, then
               10–15 minutes
Number of servings 4–6

1. Make pastry in usual way by rubbing fat into flour, adding cheese and seasonings, then enough water to make a stiff dough.
2. Roll out pastry to line an 18 cm (7 inch) flan ring and bake 'blind' in a fairly hot oven for about 15 minutes.
3. Mix filling ingredients and add enough milk to make a thick pouring consistency.
4. Pour mixture into pastry case. Bake in a warm oven for 20–25 minutes.
5. Whisk whites till stiff, fold in cheese and seasoning and spread over flan.
6. Return to a fairly hot oven for a further 10–15 minutes. Serve hot or cold with salad.

Orange Yogurt Flan

Short crust pastry:
150 g (6 oz) plain flour
¼ level teaspoon salt
37 g (1½ oz) Scottish butter
37 g (1½ oz) lard
6 teaspoons cold water to mix

Filling:
1 packet orange jelly
boiling water
2 rounded teaspoons sugar
1 (125 g or 5 oz) carton natural
  yogurt

1 medium (312 g or 11 oz) can
  mandarin oranges

Oven temperature   220°C 425°F Mark 7
Position in oven   Centre
Time in oven   20 minutes
Number of servings   6

1. Sift flour and salt, add fats and rub in
until mixture resembles fine breadcrumbs.
Add water and mix to a firm dough.
2. Roll out pastry to line a 20 cm (8 inch)
ring (fluted). Bake 'blind' in oven for 15
minutes. Remove paper or foil and continue
baking for a further 5 minutes. Cool.
3. Place jelly in a measuring jug and pour
on boiling water to make up to 250 ml (½ pint),
stir until dissolved. Place sugar in a bowl,
add half of the jelly and stir until sugar has
dissolved.
4. Add yogurt, stirring well to blend. Leave
in cool place until on point of setting. Pour
into flan case and leave to set.
5. Make remaining jelly up to 250 ml (½ pint)
with cold water. Leave in cool place until on
point of setting.
6. Drain oranges. Arrange on yogurt jelly,
pour setting jelly over oranges.
7. Decorate with fresh double cream.

Photograph shows Orange Surprise (page 69),
Yogurt Creams (page 69), Banana Parfait
(page 74), Mallow Medleys (page 71), Orange
Yogurt Flan (page 69).

Orange Surprises

5 large oranges
2 eggs, separated
50 g (2 oz) castor sugar
juice and grated rind of 1 orange
200 g (8 oz) cottage cheese, sieved
125 ml (¼ pint) fresh double cream,
  slightly whipped
12 g (½ oz) powdered gelatine,
  dissolved in 2 teaspoons water
glacé cherries and angelica for
  decoration

Number of servings   10

1. Cut each orange in half, zigzaging the
edges at same time with a sharp knife.
Release orange flesh and hollow out the
orange shells.
2. Make filling: blend egg yolks, sugar, fruit,
juices and rind in a bowl over a pan of
simmering water. Stir till mixture coats
spoon. Remove this custard and cool.
3. Blend together cheese, cream and cooled
custard. Stir dissolved gelatine into mixture.
4. When on point of setting, fold in stiffly
beaten egg whites.
5. Spoon into prepared orange shells, chill
and decorate with cherries and angelica.

Yogurt Creams

125 ml (¼ pint) fresh double cream
2 (125 g or 5 oz) cartons fruit
  yogurt
fruit for decoration

Number of servings   4

1. Whisk fresh cream until stiff.
2. Add cartons of yogurt to cream and fold
together carefully.
3. Serve in individual glass dishes and
decorate with same fruit as in yogurt.

Apricot Oyster Gâteau

Sponge:
150 g (6 oz) self raising flour
1 level teaspoon baking powder
100 g (4 oz) Scottish butter
100 g (4 oz) castor sugar
2 eggs, lightly beaten
1 tablespoon hot water

Filling:
250 ml ($\frac{1}{2}$ pint) fresh double cream
1 medium (439 g or 15$\frac{1}{2}$ oz) can
   apricots

Oven temperature   190°C 375°F Mark 5
Position in oven   Top half
Time in oven   30 minutes

1. Butter two 20 cm (8 inch) sandwich tins.
2. Sieve flour and baking powder.
3. Cream butter and sugar.
4. Add flour and eggs alternately to creamed butter and sugar and finally the hot water.
5. Divide mixture between the tins and bake in a fairly hot oven for 30 minutes.
6. When sponges have cooled whip up cream and put half into a piping bag.
7. Sandwich sponges together at an angle with remaining cream and apricots to resemble an oyster.
8. Decorate top of gâteau with stars of cream.

Syllabub

125 ml ($\frac{1}{4}$ pint) cider
2 tablespoons lemon juice
2 level teaspoons lemon peel,
   finely grated
50 g (2 oz) castor sugar
250 ml ($\frac{1}{2}$ pint) fresh double cream
brandy snaps or sponge fingers

Number of servings   6

1. Put cider, lemon juice, peel and sugar into bowl. Leave for minimum of 3 hours.
2. Add cream and whip until mixture stands in soft peaks.
3. Transfer to six sundae glasses. Leave in a cool place for several hours before serving.
4. Serve with brandy snaps or sponge fingers.

Sundae Yogurt Parfait

1 packet orange jelly
250 ml ($\frac{1}{2}$ pint) water
1 small (200 g or 8 oz) can creamed
   rice
1 (125 g or 5 oz) carton of
   mandarin and lemon yogurt
1 egg white
cream for piping
1 mandarin orange (peeled and
   segmented)

Number of servings   4

1. Place tablet of jelly and water in pan. Heat this slowly until jelly is dissolved but do not boil. Leave to cool for a few minutes.
2. Remove about 75 ml ($\frac{1}{8}$ pint) from pan and spoon into 4 sundae dishes. Leave in a cool place to set.
3. Keep remainder of jelly in a warm place to prevent from setting.
4. Stir half of remaining jelly into the creamed rice and divide mixture into the sundae glasses. Return to a cool place to set.
5. Stir remaining jelly into the yogurt. Whisk the egg white until stiff and fold into yogurt.
6. Spoon this mixture into the sundae glasses and put in cool place to set.
7. Serve topped with cream and mandarin segments.

Cream Sorbet

200 g (8 oz) sugar
750 ml (1$\frac{1}{2}$ pints) water
25 g (1 oz) lemon rind
juice of 2 lemons
250 ml ($\frac{1}{2}$ pint) fresh double cream
3 egg whites

Number of servings   7–8

1. Add sugar to water and dissolve over low heat. Reduce a little by boiling rapidly.
2. Add lemon rind and juice. Boil.
3. Strain and cool completely.
4. Whip cream and egg whites separately.
5. Stir all ingredients together.
6. Freeze.

Yogurt Surprise

1 medium (312 g or 11 oz) can
    mandarin oranges
25 g (1 oz) sultanas
50 g (2 oz) sugar
2 eggs
1 (125 g or 5 oz) carton natural
    yogurt
25 g (1 oz) plain flour, sieved
single cream for serving

Oven temperature   150°C 300°F Mark 2
Position in oven   Centre
Time in oven   Approximately 45 minutes
Number of servings   approximately 6

1. Sprinkle fruit with 25 g (1 oz) of the sugar
in an oval pie dish. Put in a low oven until
fruit is heated through.
2. Beat together until well blended the eggs,
yogurt, the remaining sugar and the
flour.
3. Spread over fruit and bake in oven until
brown and firm, approximately 45 minutes.
4. To decorate sprinkle with sugar and
serve with whipped cream.

Scotch Trifle

1 jam Swiss roll
1 medium (439 g or 15½ oz) can
    fruit cocktail
little sherry if desired
500 ml (1 pint) milk
25 g (1 oz) castor sugar
50 g (2 oz) custard powder
125 ml (¼ pint) fresh double cream

Number of servings   6–8

1. Cut up jam roll and place in base of serving
dish.
2. Drain fruit and add sherry to juice of
fruit. Reserve some pieces of fruit to decorate.
3. Pour juice mixture over jam roll and place
fruit on next.
4. Make up custard with milk, sugar and
custard powder. Cool, and pour over fruit.
5. Whisk up cream and decorate top of
custard with cream and a little of the fruit.

Mallow Medleys

250 g (10 oz) shortbread biscuits
100 g (4 oz) marshmallows
100 g (4 oz) Scottish butter
2 tablespoons milk
37 g (1½ oz) soft brown sugar
2 tablespoons sweet sherry
100 g (4 oz) cooking chocolate
2 eggs, separated
125 ml (¼ pint) fresh double cream

Number of servings   4

1. Crush biscuits between 2 sheets of greaseproof paper.
2. Cut mallows and butter into small pieces,
place in a medium saucepan with milk and
sugar. Heat gently, stir continuously till
mallows have melted. Bring to the boil,
remove from heat and cool slightly. Mix in
half of the biscuit crumbs. Mix well and divide
into individual serving dishes.
3. Place remaining crumbs in a bowl, add
sherry, mix to a paste and spread over first
layer.
4. Melt 75 g (3 oz) of the chocolate in a bowl
over boiling water.
5. Separate eggs, beat yolks into chocolate.
Whisk whites till stiff and fold into chocolate
mixture. Spoon into serving dishes and chill
till set.
6. Beat cream and pour over top of chocolate
mousse.
7. Melt 25 g (1 oz) chocolate and pipe chocolate treble clef motif on top of cream.

Raspberry Gâteau

100 g (4 oz) Scottish butter
100 g (4 oz) castor sugar
2 eggs
150 g (6 oz) self raising flour,
    sieved
1–2 dessertspoons hot water
125 ml (¼ pint) fresh double cream
fresh or frozen raspberries

Oven temperature   190°C 375°F Mark 5
Position in oven   Centre
Time in oven   25 minutes

1. Cream butter and sugar well, then add eggs and flour alternately.
2. Add a little hot water to form a soft dropping consistency.
3. Place mixture in two well buttered 18 cm (7 inch) sandwich tins.
4. Bake in a fairly hot oven for 25 minutes.
5. Whip fresh cream carefully until firm then divide cream in two. Add most of raspberries to one half of the cream and sandwich cake together with this. Pipe stars of cream on top of gâteau and decorate with raspberries.

Some Ideas for Ice Cream Sundaes

1. Vanilla ice cream, maple syrup, whirl of fresh cream topped with a walnut.
2. Vanilla ice cream, butterscotch sauce and fresh dairy cream.
3. Strawberry ice cream, strawberries and a whirl of fresh dairy cream.
4. Chocolate ice cream, chocolate sauce, fresh dairy cream topped with maraschino cherries and walnuts.
5. Coffee ice cream, coffee meringues and fresh dairy cream.
6. Coffee ice cream, maple syrup, covered with flaked nuts then topped with fresh dairy cream.
7. Vanilla ice cream, pear and chocolate sauce.

Photograph shows Raspberry Ice Cream. Meringue Nests (page 74), Raspberry Gâteau, Rich Fruit Fool.

Raspberry Ice Cream

250 ml (½ pint) fresh double cream
2 tablespoons milk
62 g (2½ oz) icing sugar, sifted
1 teaspoon vanilla essence
100 g (4 oz) raspberries, fresh,
    frozen or canned

Number of servings   4

1. Set refrigerator to coldest setting an hour before required.
2. Whisk cream and milk together until lightly stiff, mix in icing sugar and essence and pour into freezer tray.
3. Place tray in freezing compartment and leave for 45 minutes.
4. If using frozen or canned raspberries, drain thoroughly. Liquidise or sieve raspberries.
5. Take tray out of refrigerator and stir mixture thoroughly with a fork then mix in raspberries and return to freezing compartment until firm.

Rich Fruit Fool

400 g (1 lb) gooseberries, apples,
    black or redcurrants, rhubarb,
    blackberries or raspberries
3 tablespoons water
75–150 g (3–6 oz) sugar depending
    on fruit
250 ml (½ pint) fresh double cream
2 tablespoons milk
red or green food colouring
fresh cream and chopped nuts for
    decoration

Number of servings   4

1. Stew fruit according to type with water. Add sufficient sugar to sweeten, then sieve or liquidise. Leave until cool.
2. Whip cream and milk together until lightly stiff then gradually fold in fruit purée.
3. If fool is pale add some colouring.
4. Place in four sundae glasses and chill.
5. Decorate with a swirl of fresh cream and some chopped nuts.

Meringue Nests

2 egg whites
pinch of cream of tartar
100 g (4 oz) castor sugar
25 g (1 oz) granulated sugar
250 ml ($\frac{1}{2}$ pint) fresh double cream
fresh raspberries

Oven temperature   105°C 225°F Mark $\frac{1}{4}$
Position in oven   Centre
Time in oven $2\frac{1}{2}$ hours
Number of servings   4

1. Grease baking tray with cooking oil, cover with greaseproof paper and brush with more oil.
2. Place egg whites in bowl, add a pinch of cream of tartar and whisk until stiff.
3. Add half of the castor sugar. Continue to whisk until meringue stands in firm peaks. Add remaining castor sugar and whisk until very stiff then slowly fold in granulated sugar.
4. Pipe circles of meringue on baking tray to form bases of baskets then pipe rosettes round the edge to make the sides. Bake in a cool oven for $2\frac{1}{2}$ hours until dried out.
5. When cold, fill with whipped cream and decorate with raspberries.

Banana Parfait

1 packet lemon jelly
250 ml ($\frac{1}{2}$ pint) boiling water
1 family size block (425 ml or
   17 fl oz) vanilla ice cream
2 bananas
125 ml ($\frac{1}{4}$ pint) fresh double cream,
   whipped

Number of servings   8

1. Dissolve jelly in boiling water.
2. Cut ice cream into small pieces, stir into hot jelly.
3. When nearly set, fold in sliced bananas.
4. Pour into glass bowl.
5. Serve with whipped cream.

Strawberry Shortcake

Shortcake:
200 g (8 oz) plain flour
2 level teaspoons baking powder
50 g (2 oz) Scottish butter
25 g (1 oz) castor sugar
1 egg
milk to mix

Filling:
200 g ($\frac{1}{2}$ lb) strawberries
250 ml ($\frac{1}{2}$ pint) cream
little castor sugar for berries

Oven temperature   230°C 450°F Mark 8
Position in oven   Top half
Time in oven   15–20 minutes
Number of servings   6

1. Butter a 20 cm (8 inch) round cake tin.
2. Sift together flour and baking powder, rub in butter, add castor sugar.
3. Mix to a stiff dough with egg and a little milk.
4. Knead lightly until smooth. Shape into a round shape about 19 cm ($7\frac{1}{2}$ inches) across. Place in prepared cake tin. Bake in a very hot oven for 15–20 minutes until golden brown and firm to the touch.
5. Cool slightly then remove from tin and split in two across. Place on a wire rack to cool completely.
Filling:
6. Hull and wash strawberries and slice about two thirds of them.
7. Beat up cream and place the sliced strawberries in half of the cream with a little castor sugar.
8. Fill shortcake and decorate top of cake with cream and whole strawberries.

Coffee Mallow Cream

200 g (8 oz) marshmallows
250 ml (½ pint) milk
2 tablespoons instant coffee
    powder
125 ml (¼ pint) fresh double cream,
    whipped
25 g (1 oz) chopped nuts

Number of servings   4

1. Put marshmallows, milk and coffee powder in a bowl and dissolve over a pan of boiling water. Leave to cool.
2. When beginning to set, fold in half of the whipped cream and most of the chopped nuts.
3. Pour into individual sundae dishes and leave to set.
4. Decorate with remaining cream and nuts.

Dairy Ice Cream

4 eggs, separated
100 g (4 oz) icing sugar, sieved
250 ml (½ pint) fresh double cream
¼ teaspoon vanilla essence

Number of servings   6

1. Set refrigerator to freezing.
2. Whisk egg yolks till light and creamy. Whisk whites till stiff then gradually whisk in sugar.
3. Whip up cream.
4. Add vanilla essence to yolks, fold in egg whites then whipped cream.
5. Turn into freezer tray and freeze for one hour.
6. Stir well with fork and refreeze for 2–3 hours.
N.B. Instead of vanilla the following flavourings may be substituted:
3 tablespoons coffee essence
100 g (4 oz) grated chocolate or
200 g (8 oz) puréed fruit

Butterscotch Sauce

50 g (2 oz) Scottish butter
50 g (2 oz) soft brown sugar
2 tablespoons golden syrup
1 small can condensed milk

1. Place butter, sugar and syrup in a double saucepan and heat gently until sugar has melted.
2. Add condensed milk. Cook for a further 2–3 minutes, stirring all the time.
3. Serve either hot or cold with ice cream.

Crème Brûlée

250 ml (½ pint) milk
250 ml (½ pint) single cream
6 egg yolks
25 g (1 oz) castor sugar
¼ teaspoon vanilla essence
2 tablespoons demerara sugar

Number of servings   5

1. Heat milk and cream to just below boiling point.
2. Beat egg yolks, add sugar.
3. Add milk and cream slowly to eggs, cook in a pan over a low heat until sauce thickens.
4. Add essence.
5. Put in an ovenproof dish and chill, preferably overnight.
6. Sprinkle with demerara sugar and grill until sugar turns a deep brown.

Black Forest Gâteau

150 g (6 oz) self raising flour
2 level tablespoons drinking
  chocolate
2 eggs, beaten
100 g (4 oz) Scottish butter
100 g (4 oz) castor sugar
1–2 dessertspoons hot water

Filling:
200 g (8 oz) fresh double cream
75 g (3 oz) maraschino cherries

Oven temperature   190°C 375°F Mark 5
Position in oven   Centre
Time in oven   25 minutes

1. Butter two 18 cm (7 inch) round sandwich tins.
2. Sieve flour and chocolate powder. Beat eggs.
3. Cream butter and sugar, add eggs and flour mixture alternately and finally add a little hot water to give a soft mixture.
4. Divide mixture into prepared tins.
5. Bake in a fairly hot oven for 25 minutes.
6. When cool, make up filling by whisking fresh cream until stiff enough to pipe. Halve cream and to one half add the cherries. Sandwich sponges together with this mixture. Pipe the remainder of cream on top and decorate with the rest of the cherries.

Quickie Cream Cakes

fresh double cream
1 slice of Swiss roll per cake
1 medium (312 g or 11 oz) can
  mandarin oranges
1 packet chocolate buttons

1. Pipe fresh double cream on to slices of Swiss roll.
2. Decorate with mandarin oranges and chocolate buttons.
3. Other fruits can be used, also cherries, nuts and angelica.

Photograph shows Black Forest Gâteau, Quickie Cream Cakes, Buttered Shortbread, Fruit Loaf.

Butter Shortbread

150 g (6 oz) plain flour
pinch of salt
100 g (4 oz) Scottish butter
50 g (2 oz) castor sugar

Oven temperature   150°C 300°F Mark 2
Position in oven   Centre
Time in oven   1 hour

1. Add salt to flour.
2. Cream butter and sugar well.
3. Gradually work the flour into creamed mixture and knead until smooth.
4. Form mixture into a round or oblong shape about 1 cm (½ inch) thick.
5. Place on baking tin, prick and decorate edges with knife.
6. Bake in oven until golden brown.
7. Cut into required size of pieces when still hot then cool on a cooling tray.

Fruit Loaf

100 g (4 oz) Scottish butter
125 ml (¼ pint) water
100 g (4 oz) raisins
100 g (4 oz) sultanas
200 g (8 oz) self raising flour
100 g (4 oz) castor sugar
2 eggs, beaten
2 level teaspoons bicarbonate of
  soda

Oven temperature   180°C 350°F Mark 4
Position in oven   Centre
Time in oven   45 minutes at 180°C 350°F
                Mark 4
                15 minutes at 150°C 300°F
                Mark 2

1. Melt butter in pan, add water, raisins and sultanas and boil for five minutes.
2. Mix in the flour, sugar, eggs and bicarbonate of soda.
3. Place in greased loaf tin and bake in a moderate oven for 45 minutes then reduce heat for 15 minutes.

Russian Cherry Cake

1 packet blackcurrant jelly
400 g (1 lb) stoned cherries
18–20 sponge finger biscuits
250 ml (½ pint) fresh double cream
200 g (8 oz) Scottish cheddar
   cheese, finely grated

Number of servings   6–8

1. Dissolve jelly in 250 ml (½ pint) of boiling water. Pour ½ cm (¼ inch) layer of jelly into the base of an 18 or 20 cm (7 or 8 inch) cake tin (about 1½ litre or 2 pint capacity).
2. Leave jelly to set then decorate this layer of jelly with about 10 cherries.
3. Place the biscuits side by side round the tin with the curved side of the biscuits facing the tin.
4. Whisk cream until thick, fold in cheese and remaining cherries and stir in remaining cooled jelly.
5. Pour into the cake tin and leave to set in refrigerator.
6. When the mixture is set, trim biscuits to level of mixture, dip base of tin in hot water and turn out on plate.
7. Decorate with cream if desired.

Mandarin Cheesecake

50 g (2 oz) Scottish butter
8 digestive biscuits, crushed
125 ml (¼ pint) fresh double cream
200 g (8 oz) cream cheese
50 g (2 oz) icing sugar
125 ml (¼ pint) milk
1 medium (312 g or 11 oz) can
   mandarin oranges

Number of servings   5–6

1. Melt butter and add crushed biscuits.
2. Press mixture into round flat dish.
3. Whip cream and reserve half for decoration.
4. Cream the cheese and slowly add all icing sugar.
5. Gradually beat in the milk.
6. Fold in half of the cream.
7. Put mixture on top of flan base, spread evenly.
8. Drain juice from mandarin oranges and use the oranges and remaining cream to decorate.

Yogurt Cake

1 (125 g or 5 oz) carton yogurt
   (any flavour)
150 g (6 oz) Scottish butter,
   softened
100 g (4 oz) castor sugar
3 eggs
300 g (12 oz) self raising flour

Oven temperature   180°C 350°F Mark 4
Position in oven   ⅔ from top
Time in oven   45–55 minutes

1. Grease an 18 cm (7 inch) round, deep cake tin or two 18 cm (7 inch) sandwich tins.
2. Put all ingredients in bowl and beat together with a wooden spoon for 2 to 3 minutes or use an electric mixer.
3. Turn into prepared tin or tins, and bake in a preheated oven as above.
4. Serve the large cake as a cut cake, or fill sandwich cakes with jam and butter icing.

Coffee Cream Puffs

Choux pastry:
62 g (2½ oz) plain flour
pinch of salt
125 ml (¼ pint) water
50 g (2 oz) Scottish butter
2 standard eggs, well beaten

Oven temperature   205°C 400°F Mark 6
Position in oven   Centre
Time in oven   30–35 minutes
Number of cakes   9

1. Sieve flour and salt twice.
2. Put water and butter in pan, heat until butter melts, then bring to brisk boil.
3. Lower heat, add all the flour. Stir briskly until mixture forms soft ball and leaves sides of pan clean.
4. Cool slightly, and add eggs very gradually, beating hard till mixture is smooth, shiny and firm enough to stand in soft peaks.
5. Pipe or spoon equal amounts of mixture, well apart, onto buttered tray.
6. Bake in centre of a hot oven for 10 minutes, then reduce to moderate (180°C 355°F Mark 4) for further 20–25 minutes.
7. Remove from oven and quickly make a slit round side of each puff.
8. Return to oven for 5 minutes to dry out.
9. Cool on wire rack.

To make into coffee cream puffs:
250 ml (½ pint) fresh double cream
coffee glacé icing
pieces of walnut

Whip cream till thick, fill puffs with cream, cover tops with icing and pieces of walnut.

Cheese and Nut Loaf

200 g (8 oz) walnuts
75 g (3 oz) Scottish cheddar
** cheese, finely grated**
1 medium onion, finely grated
150 g (6 oz) fresh brown
** breadcrumbs**
2 level teaspoons salt
2 level tablespoons parsley,
** finely chopped**
5 tablespoons hot milk
1 level teaspoon mustard
1 level tablespoon tomato paste
pepper to taste
12 g (½ oz) Scottish butter

Oven temperature   180°C 350°F Mark 4
Position in oven   Centre
Time in oven   45 minutes

1. Line baking tray with foil and butter lightly.
2. Grind nuts finely and put in bowl, add finely grated cheese and onion.
3. Add all remaining ingredients except butter and mix thoroughly.
4. Shape into a loaf 7½ cm (3 inches) high and stand it on prepared tray.
5. Dot top with flakes of butter and bake in centre of oven.
6. Cut into slices and serve with mustard or tomato sauce.

Choc-au-lait

1 glass milk
2 teaspoons chocolate milk shake
    powder
a little coffee essence or instant
    coffee

Whisk all ingredients together using chilled milk.

Chocolate Mallow Float

1 mug hot milk
3 teaspoons drinking chocolate
    powder
1 or 2 marshmallows

Heat milk and pour into mug. Sprinkle chocolate powder into milk and stir well. Float one or two marshmallows on top.

Strawberry Fizz

strawberry milk shake syrup
125 ml ($\frac{1}{4}$ pint) milk
lemonade

Place a little strawberry syrup in glass, add milk, stir and top up with lemonade.

Pineapple Frappé

1 glass cold milk
pineapple milk shake syrup
1 tablespoon ice cream or
    whipped fresh cream
chocolate vermicelli to decorate

1. Pour a glass of cold milk and add milk shake syrup.
2. Top with a scoop of ice cream or cream and decorate with chocolate vermicelli.

Ginger Lime Fizz

milk
lime milk shake syrup
ginger beer

Pour two-thirds of a glass of milk, add a little milk shake syrup, and top up with ginger beer.

Open Sandwiches

Base – French bread
    Vienna bread
    Rye bread
    Crispbread for slimmers
    Finger rolls or small round rolls
    Cheese scones

Topping – thick layer of Scottish
    butter, then base of lettuce
    followed by some of the following:
1. Grated cheese – can be mixed
    with fresh cream and salad
    cream
2. Tomato
3. Cucumber
4. Hardboiled egg
5. Shrimps or prawns with a
    cream dressing
6. Sardines
7. Cottage cheese
8. Pineapple, mandarin oranges
9. Nuts
10. Gammon or other cold meat
11. Red or green peppers
12. Parsley

N.B. It is essential to use a generous layer of butter for an open sandwich so that the topping can be kept firmly in place.

6. Children's Cookery

All the recipes in this section are fun to cook and have easy to follow step-by-step instructions. Before you begin you should read the notes below.

Before you start cooking

1. Wash your hands.
2. Put on a clean apron.
3. Collect your utensils.
4. Gather your ingredients.
5. If using an oven switch it on. If in any doubt as to how to use the oven, ask an adult to help you.
6. Read your recipe and make sure you understand it.

Safety Precautions

1. Be very careful not to cut yourself when using sharp knives.
2. Always chop on a chopping board.
3. Pan handles should be turned inwards to reduce risk of them being spilled or knocked off the stove.
4. Always keep a First Aid kit handy, and know how to deal with cuts, burns and scalds.

Cheese and Sausage Bake

You will need:
400 g (1 lb) potatoes
200 g (½ lb) onions
25 g (1 oz) Scottish butter
300 g (12 oz) sliced or link sausages
150 g (6 oz) Scottish cheddar cheese,
grated
salt and pepper
3 tablespoons milk
Serves 4

1. Peel potatoes and bring to boil in salted water. Simmer until tender, about 30 minutes.

2. Drain and steam them dry.

3. When potatoes have cooled a little, slice them.

4. Peel the onions and slice them. Melt the butter in a frying pan, add the onions and fry over a low heat for 5 minutes.

5. Add sausages to frying pan and fry on both sides until cooked.

6. Arrange potatoes, onions, cheese and sausages in layers in an ovenproof dish, seasoning each layer.

7. Pour milk over dish, then bake in a fairly hot oven (190°C 375°F Mark 5) for 20–25 minutes.

Macaroni Cheese

You will need:
50 g (2 oz) macaroni
1 level teaspoon salt
25 g (1 oz) butter
25g (1 oz) flour
250 ml (½ pint) milk
75 g (3 oz) Scottish Cheddar cheese, grated
little salt and pepper
½ level teaspoon mustard
tomato slices and parsley for garnish
Serves 4

1. Measure about 1 litre (1½ pints) water into a pan, add the salt and bring to the boil. Put macaroni into boiling salted water and boil until soft, about 10 minutes.

2. Place butter in a medium-sized saucepan and melt slowly.

3. Take pan off heat, add flour and mix in well. Gradually pour in milk, a little at a time, stirring well with a wooden spoon.

5. Grate cheese. Add most of the grated cheese and seasoning and stir for 2–3 minutes.

4. Return pan to heat and bring to boil, stirring all the time.

7. Add macaroni to cheese sauce and mix well.

6. When macaroni is cooked, drain water carefully through sieve.

8. Place macaroni cheese in an ovenproof dish. Sprinkle remaining grated cheese on top. Place dish under grill for a short time to brown lightly.

9. Garnish dish with slices of tomato and a sprig of parsley. Now enjoy it!

Country Salad

You will need:
1 lettuce
2 red apples
100 g (4 oz) Scottish cheddar cheese
100 g (4 oz) spam or ham
1 small can pineapple cubes
125 ml (¼ pint) fresh double cream
salt and pepper
50 g (2 oz) sultanas
cucumber and tomato to garnish
Serves 4

1. Wash lettuce carefully and drain off water.

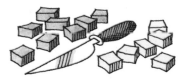

3. Cut up cheese and spam to same size of pieces.

2. Quarter apples, remove cores and cut into 1 cm (½ inch) dice.

5. Place cream in a bowl and whip it up lightly, adding a little seasoning if desired.

4. Open can of pineapple and drain off juice.

6. Add apple, cheese, spam or ham, pineapple cubes and sultanas to cream and toss well together.

7. Arrange lettuce round a salad bowl and place salad mixture in centre. Garnish with slices of cucumber and wedges of tomato.

Gammon, Cheese and Pineapple

You will need:
4 gammon steaks
little Scottish butter
4 pineapple rings
4 slices Scottish Cheddar cheese
parsley
Serves 4

1. Brush gammon steaks with butter and grill on both sides until cooked.

2. Place a pineapple ring on top of each steak, then cover with a slice of cheese.

3. Grill until cheese has melted and pineapple is heated through.

4. Remove from grill onto serving dish with a fish slice. Serve garnished with parsley.

Banana Cream

You will need:
bananas
½ teaspoon lemon juice
125 ml (¼ pint) fresh double cream
2 egg whites
1 (125 g or 5 oz) carton plain yogurt
75 g (3 oz) castor sugar
chocolate flake bar to decorate
Serves 4–6

1. Mash up bananas on a plate and add lemon juice.

2. Empty cream into a bowl and whip up with a rotary whisk until quite stiff.

3. Mix bananas into cream and add yogurt.

4. Whip up egg whites in a different bowl till stiff, then add sugar.

5. Fold egg whites carefully into banana mixture.

6. Pour into individual dishes or in a large bowl, and decorate with broken chocolate flake.

Chocolate Tiffin

You will need:
200 g (8 oz) digestive biscuits
50 g (2 oz) glacé cherries
100 g (4 oz) Scottish butter
3 level tablespoons syrup
25g (1 oz) drinking chocolate
150 g (6 oz) cooking chocolate for top

1. Line a 18 × 20 × 2cm (7 × 8 × 1 inch) baking tin with greaseproof paper or foil and grease lightly.

2. Crush biscuits by placing in a bag and crushing with a rolling pin.

3. Chop cherries.

4. Melt butter and syrup in pan.

5. Place crushed biscuits in a bowl, add drinking chocolate, fruit and melted butter and syrup; mix well.

6. Place mixture in prepared tin and press down well. Leave in a cool place or refrigerator to set for about an hour.

7. Melt cooking chocolate carefully in a bowl over a pan of boiling water. When melted, pour over mixture in tin and spread evenly.

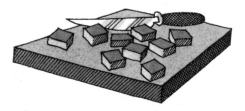

8. When set, pull out tiffin with paper, remove from paper and cut into required size.

Golf Balls

You will need:
125 g (5 oz) coconut
75 g (3 oz) porridge oats
50 g (2 oz) drinking chocolate
50 g (2 oz) Scottish butter
3 tablespoons milk
75 g (3 oz) sugar
1 small packet marshmallows
chocolate vermicelli
Makes 14–16

1. Mix together coconut, porridge oats and drinking chocolate in a large bowl.

2. Melt butter, milk and sugar in a pan.

3. Pour melted mixture over dry ingredients and mix together. Leave to firm up.

4. Cut marshmallows into quarters.

5. When mixture is firm, form round pieces of marshmallow.

6. Roll Golf Balls in chocolate vermicelli. Place in paper cases.

Fruit Cream Sundae

You will need:
1 small can fruit cocktail
500 ml (1 pint) milk
1 packet Instant Whip
little fresh double cream
nuts or cherries for decoration
Serves 4

1. Open can and strain juice from fruit.

2. Place fruit in 4 individual dishes.

3. Pour the milk into a large bowl. Add Instant Whip to milk and whisk for 1 minute.

5. Whisk up a little fresh cream carefully (read page 11).

4. Pour mixture over fruit in dishes. Leave to set.

7. Decorate each sweet with a swirl of cream, then place a piece of nut or cherry on top of the cream.

6. Place in piping bag with a star shaped nozzle.

Crunchy Chiffon Pie

You will need:
50 g (2 oz) Scottish butter
3 level dessertspoons syrup
150 g (6 oz) digestive biscuits
1 packet Angel Delight
250 ml (½ pint) milk
125 ml (¼ pint) fresh double cream
chocolate flake bar to decorate
Serves 6

1. Melt butter and syrup in a pan.

2. Put digestive biscuits in a paper bag and crush with a rolling pin.

3. Pour crushed biscuits into pan and mix well.

4. Place mixture in a flan ring and press mixture with a wooden spoon to the shape of the flan. Put in a cool place or a refrigerator to set.

5. When flan has set, remove flan ring carefully and place on a plate. Make up Angel Delight with milk according to the instructions on packet and pour into flan.

6. Whisk up double cream carefully and either spoon it onto the flan or pipe it as a decoration.

7. Break up chocolate flake and sprinkle some on top of flan.

Cheese Scones

You will need:
200 g (8 oz) self raising flour
1 level teaspoon salt
a little pepper
$\frac{1}{4}$ level teaspoon mustard
1 level teaspoon baking powder
100 g (4 oz) Scottish cheddar cheese
1 egg } together to make up to just over
milk } 125 ml ($\frac{1}{4}$ pint)
25 g (1 oz) Scottish butter
Makes 8–10

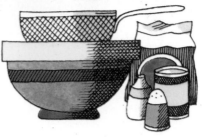

1. Sieve all dry ingredients together into a mixing bowl.

2. Grate cheese.

3. Whisk egg and add milk to make a generous 125 ml ($\frac{1}{4}$ pint).

4. Rub butter into dry ingredients until it resembles fine breadcrumbs.

5. Mix in cheese, then stir in milk and egg thoroughly with a knife.

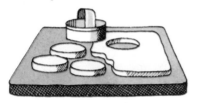

6. Place mixture onto a floured board, roll out to about 1 cm ($\frac{1}{2}$ inch) thick, and cut into scones.

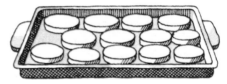

7. Place on baking tray which has been dusted with flour.

8. Place on the top shelf of a very hot oven (230°C 450°F Mark 8) and bake for 10 minutes.

9. Take out of oven and place on a wire cooling tray. Serve with plenty of Scottish butter.

Fresh Cream Angel Cakes

You will need:
100 g (4 oz) self raising flour
2 eggs
100 g (4 oz) Scottish butter, softened
100 g (4 oz) castor sugar
125 ml (¼ pint) fresh double cream
Makes 16

1. Sieve flour into a bowl and beat eggs in another bowl.

3. Place softened butter and sugar in a mixing bowl, and beat with a wooden spoon until soft and creamy. Beat in the eggs and 2 level tablespoons of the flour.

2. Place about 16 paper cases in ungreased bun tins.

4. Fold in remainder of flour with a metal spoon, then place a heaped teaspoonful of mixture into each paper case.

5. Bake in the top half of a fairly hot oven (190°C 375°F Mark 5) for 20–25 minutes.

6. When cooked, place on a cooling tray.

7. When cool, cut a round from top of cake then cut in half to form 'wings'. Pipe or spoon some whipped cream on top, then replace 'wings' and dust with icing sugar.

Index